The Development of the Inca State

The Development of the Inca State

By Brian S. Bauer

Foreword by Gary Urton

University of Texas Press   Austin

Requests for permission to reproduce material from this
work should be sent to Permissions, University of Texas
Press, Box 7819, Austin, TX 78713–7819.

⊗ The paper used in this publication meets the minimum
requirements of American National Standard for
Information Sciences—Permanence of Paper for Printed
Library Materials, ANSI Z39, 48–1984.

Library of Congress Cataloging-in-Publication Data

Bauer, Brian S.
    The development of the Inca state / Brian S. Bauer : foreword by
Gary Urton. — 1st ed.
        p.   cm.
    Includes bibliographical references and index.
    ISBN 0-292-70848-3 (pbk.)
        1. Incas—Politics and government. 2. Incas—Social conditions. 3.
    Incas—Economic conditions. 4. Social classes—Peru—Cuzco Region—
    History. 5. Cuzco Region (Peru)—Antiquities. 6. Peru—Antiquities. I.
    Title.
    F3429.1.C9B38   1992
    985′.01—dc20   91-40030

To
L. J. Skaggs and Mary C. Skaggs
in gratitude
for their encouragement and support

Contents

Plates

Maps

Figures

Contents

Tables

Foreword
by
Gary Urton

OF THE THREE high civilizations of the pre-Columbian Americas—the Aztecan, Mayan and Incan—few scholars would dispute that we know more about the history and the historical development of the Middle American states than we do about the Inca. However, the surprising and initially unsettling message that comes through clearly in this ground-breaking study by Brian Bauer is that, in fact, we know even less about the history of the development of the Inca Empire than has traditionally been supposed. In addition to explaining why this is the case, Bauer goes on to lay the groundwork for a new theory of the initial stages of the evolution of the Inca state in the heartland of the empire—the region in the immediate environs of the Inca capital, Cuzco, Peru. In both pulling down the castle of cards on which the traditional theory of the origins of the Inca state in the Cuzco Valley was built and replacing the theory with a new one—grounded in ethnic differentiation and alliances, ecological complementarity, and other archaeologically and ethnohistorically well-attested Andean institutions and modes of interaction—Bauer has succeeded in returning to archaeology its (rightful) place of primacy in the investigation of the origins and initial phases of the evolution of the Inca Empire.

As is well known, the Aztec and Maya developed systems of hieroglyphic writing and calendrical notations centuries before the arrival of the Europeans. On the basis of this native documentation, supplemented by decades of scientific archaeological and ethnohistorical studies, the general contours of the course that events took in Middle American pre-Columbian history are slowly becoming known to scholars and the general public. The Inca, on the other hand, appear not to have developed a system of writing, or, if they did, we have not yet succeeded in either identifying it or deciphering any indigenous historical narratives that such a system might contain. The only historical narratives available to us for Inca civilization are those contained in the documents written by European soldiers, clergymen, and bureaucrats in the years following the Spanish conquest of the Inca Empire, beginning in 1532. Through the careful and critical study of the information in the Spanish chronicles pertaining to the supposed history of the Inca Empire, a tradition of interpretation has built up over the years since the 1940s (without, I would add, any support from the archaeological record in the Cuzco Valley), which asserts that, while early Inca history is lost in the mists of mythology, true history—that is, history built on a framework of an absolute chronology (albeit one deduced solely from the narratives contained in the Spanish chronicles)—begins with the accession to the throne of a young Inca prince, Pachacuti Inca Yupanqui, in the late 1430s. The galvanizing event of this historicized representation of the narratives contained in the Spanish chronicles was a war between the Inca and their arch-rivals, the Chanca. Following the defeat of the Chanca, the Inca state was reorganized and there began what was destined to be a relentless expansion of the state, propelled by the genius of the young king, Pachacuti Inca Yupanqui, out of the Cuzco Valley to the four quarters of the world to produce the Inca Empire, which was known by the Inca as Tahuantinsuyu ("the four parts together").

With the above scenario as the central paradigm guiding the thinking of students of Andean cultural history over the past half-century—a paradigm built on a literal reading of the chronicles supplemented by the results of the relatively meager archaeological work that was undertaken on the origins of the Inca state in the immediate environs of the city of Cuzco, which seemed to confirm the abrupt appearance and expansion of the state in late pre-Hispanic times—there was little inducement for archaeologists to undertake systematic investigations on the origins of the Inca state in the immediate circum-Cuzco region. Rather, what the dominant paradigm seemed to call for was, first, descriptive studies of fully evolved Inca culture in and around Cuzco and, second, an accounting of the means whereby the more distant populations of the "hinterland" were incorporated into the Inca state. Such studies are well represented in the literature on Inca civilization.

While drawing on these two types of studies in the present work, what Bauer does beyond that—and this is the original contribution of this study—is to confront the original paradigm with the results of an archaeological survey and some excavations, carried out from 1984 to 1987 within 600 square kilometers of territory in the Province of Paruro, south of Cuzco. One of the considerations that led Bauer to focus his research on this part of the territory around Cuzco is that the site of

Maukallaqta, the site the Inca appear to have recognized as "Pacariqtambo," the place of origin of the first Inca king, lies within this region.

As Bauer demonstrates, the ceramic sequences and settlement pattern profiles from the Province of Paruro *contradict* the model of Inca state formation based on the event of the Chanca war, in the late 1430s, and the organizational genius of a single person, Pachacuti Inca Yupanqui. Instead, Bauer's survey data strongly suggest that the Inca emerged as the central and dominant power of the Cuzco region during the Killke Period (A.D. 1000–1400), several centuries earlier than previously supposed. Furthermore, not only is there no evidence of warfare or ethnic conflict in the Province of Paruro during Killke or Inca times (as the Spanish chronicles assert was the case), but also there is a strong pattern of continuity in the subsistence-settlement systems—including moiety divisions—from the Killke Period to the Inca Period. Clearly, if Bauer's research is confirmed by future studies, we will need to develop a new set of theories and a new guiding paradigm to explain the initial phases of the development of the Inca state in and around Cuzco.

Finally, I would point out that this book ought to be read as an enormously liberating and, at the same time, challenging work for students of Andean social and cultural history. It is liberating because it removes the props of pseudohistory from the foundations of Inca studies. But in that act of liberation, new challenges emerge; these involve the challenge of not only formulating new theories to explain the origins and evolution of the Inca Empire and its relationship to earlier highland and coastal cultures, but also finding a new accommodation between archaeology and the rich and valuable information on the Inca Empire contained in the Spanish chronicles. This study takes initial, important steps in both these directions.

Acknowledgments

MANY INDIVIDUALS and organizations contributed to the completion of this study. I am grateful to my doctoral committee at the University of Chicago who provided academic guidance and practical advice at all stages of the project. Don Rice and Alan Kolata both served as chairpersons and contributed to the development of the work. I am equally grateful to Gary Urton, who shared with me his ethnographic and ethnohistorical information from the region of Pacariqtambo and who provided advice both in the field and while I was writing the manuscript. This work has profited from the critical readings provided by Jane Buikstra, Gordon McEwan, Jeffrey Parsons, Terence Turner, and Tom Zuidema. Various chapters have been read by Karen Chávez, Sergio Chávez, Terence D'Altroy, Ann Kendall, and Charles Stanish, as well as by Peter Burgi, Marianne Carr, Paul Goldstein, Clare Leader, John Meloy, and Karen Wise. Their criticisms and suggestions are gratefully acknowledged. I also owe much to Sara Lunt, who aided me in developing the ceramic descriptions presented in this work.

Permission for this project was granted by the Instituto Nacional de Cultura (INC): Lima and Cuzco (Resolución Suprema No. 145-86-ED). The members of the INC in Cuzco, including Oscar Nuñez del Prado C., Arminda Gibaja Oviedo, Wilfredo Yepez Valdez, Ruben Orellana Neira, and Percy Ardiles Nieves, were particularly helpful. Members of the Cuzco academic community also aided me over the course of this study. I would especially like to thank Luis Barreda Murillo and Alfredo Valencia Zegarra, who gave me much support during my stays in Cuzco, as well as José Gonzales Corrales, Italo Oberti Rodríguez, and Manuel Chávez Ballón.

Over the four years of fieldwork for this project many people, including Melissa Baker, Tamara Bray, Leslie Ranken, Silvia Lopez Aranquri,

Eliana Gamarra Carrillo, Carmen Jurado Carrasco, Wilbert Torres Poblete, Wilbert Vera Robles, Edmundo de la Vega, Yolanda Vargas Chacón, Miriam Caceres Gallegos, Sonia Dianderas Medina, and Marlene Piñares, aided me in surveying, excavating, and processing the artifacts. René Barreto, Enrique Castelo Olivares, Julia Meyerson, Nilo Torres Poblete, and Ernesto Quispe Sarasi drew many of the figures in this study.

The people of the Province of Paruro kindly allowed the project to be conducted across their fields and welcomed us into their communities. I became particularly close to the Flores family of Mollebamba, Mario Huamani of Yaurisque, Baltizar Quispe of Pacariqtambo, and Narciso Villacorte and Inez Sanchez at Ccoipa. A special thanks goes to the members of Mollebamba, a community near the ruins of Maukallaqta, for their hospitality and support during my many visits to the site. I would like to thank, furthermore, the members of the many different communities in which we lived during the course of the fieldwork, including Yaurisque, Pumate, Pacariqtambo, Pirca, Huanoquite, Paruro, Ccoipa, Cusibamba Alto, Colcha, Araypallpa, San Lorenzo, Ccochirhuay, Pillpinto, Accha, and Omacha, and the members of the Hotel Imperio in Cuzco.

Sections of this work have appeared in earlier publications. Part of Chapter 5, which reviews the history of Killke research, has appeared in an article by Charles Stanish and myself in *Fieldiana*. Sections of Chapter 8 that discuss the moiety organization of the Pacariqtambo region appeared in an article in the *Revista Andina*, while sections of Chapter 7 have appeared in *Ñawpa Pacha* and *Latin American Antiquity*.

The research presented in this work was conducted through the generous support of foundations, corporations, and individuals. Major funding was provided by the L. J. Skaggs and Mary C. Skaggs Foundation, the Organization of American States, the Fulbright-Hays fellowship committee, and the University of Chicago Housing System. Their assistance is gratefully acknowledged. Equipment and support were also provided by the American Can Foundation, the Institute for New World Archaeology, Brunton Corporation, Moss Tent, Texas Instruments, Fuji U.S.A., and Koh-I-Noor Rapidograph. Barbara Crane, Phillip Weaver, John Folger, and Gayle and William Bauer played special roles in supporting this project. Finally, I express my gratitude to Martina Munsters, who supported and accompanied me through all stages of this project.

Y que el tiempo consume la memoria de las cosas de tal manera, que si no es por rastros y vías exquisitas, en lo venidero no se sabe con verdadera noticia lo que pasó. (Pedro de Cieza de León [1553])

And because time consumes the memory of things in such a way that if it were not for impressions and clues, in the future one would not know what actually happened in the past.

1.
Introduction

THE CUZCO VALLEY is located in the south-central Andes of Peru at an altitude of 3,300 meters above sea level (masl).[1] This fertile valley emerged preeminent in the fifteenth century A.D. as the heartland of the Inca. Near the north end of the valley lies the city of Cuzco, the sacred capital of the Inca state and the royal seat for the dynastic order that ruled over it. The region immediately surrounding the Valley of Cuzco, the Cuzco region, was occupied by a number of different ethnic groups that were absorbed into the Inca state during the early period of state formation.[2] This work begins to examine the processes of Inca state development that occurred in the Cuzco region between the Killke Period (A.D. 1000–1400) and the Inca Period (A.D. 1400–1532), as experienced by three ethnic groups occupying an area directly south of the imperial capital.[3]

Current Theories of Inca State Development

At the time of the Spanish invasion in 1532, the Inca Empire was the largest state in the Americas. With its political center in the Cuzco Valley, the empire controlled much of the area included within the modern nations of Ecuador, Peru, Chile, and Bolivia (Map 1). The expansion of the Inca from a Cuzco power, beginning sometime in the late fourteenth or early fifteenth century, to a pan-Andean one at the time of European contact is suggested through a number of related accounts. The legend most frequently recorded by the Spaniards states that the Inca spread rapidly beyond the confines of the Cuzco Valley under the leadership of Viracocha Inca and his son Pachacuti Inca Yupanqui. The catalyst for sudden political growth in the Cuzco region is said to have been the Inca's ability to unify the various ethnic

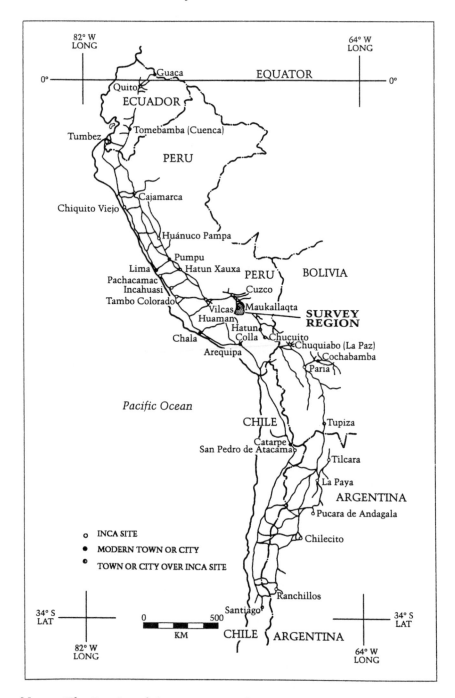

Map 1. The Empire of the Inca, 1531 (after Hyslop 1990:275)

groups of the region and a decisive military victory that this Cuzco-based alliance achieved over a traditional rival, the Chanca. In the general absence of systematically collected archaeological survey data from the Cuzco region, questions concerning the early emergence of the Inca state have been approached primarily through the examination of this legendary account.

The Spanish chronicles suggest that, before the reign of Viracocha Inca, the Cuzco region was inhabited by various competing ethnic polities. It is said that regional alliances were shifting continuously during this era of prestate conflict and that the population lived under a constant fear of raids. For example, Sarmiento de Gamboa writes:

> Y era tanto lo que cada pueblo pugnaba por su libertad con sus cinchis y sin ellos, queste procuraba subjetar á aquel y el otro al otro, especialmente en el tiempo de los ingas, que aun dentro del mesmo Cuzco los de un arrabal, llamado Carmenga, traían guerra con los de otro arrabal, llamado Cayocache. Y así ha de entender, que . . . los siete ingas predecesores de Viracocha Inga, aunque por el poder que tenían de los ayllos, tenían temorizados á los del Cuzco y algunos de los muy cercanos del Cuzco, no les duraba más el servirlos, de cuanto les tenían la lanza encima, porque al momento que podían, se acogían á las armas, apellidando libertad; la cual aunque con gran riesgo y muertes sustentaron, aún los de dentro del Cuzco, hasta el tiempo del Viracocha Inga. (Sarmiento de Gamboa [1572, Chap. 24] 1906:56–57)

Each town struggled so much for its freedom with and without its *cinchis* (leaders) that each tried to subjugate the others, especially in the time of the Inca; even in Cuzco itself those of one section, called Carmenca, waged war with those of another section, called Cayocache. And although it needs to be understood . . . that the seven Inca predecessors of Viracocha Inca had those of Cuzco and its surroundings terrorized, through the power given to them by the *ayllus* (kin groups), the Inca's control of them only lasted while the Inca had their weapons on them, because the instant the subjugated could, they took to arms and demanded freedom, which was risky since even those within Cuzco died. This went on until the time of Viracocha Inca.[4]

According to the heroic narratives presented in the chronicles, this chaotic period of regional hostilities ended abruptly during the reign of Viracocha Inca when the Chanca, an aggressive ethnic group located in the modern Department of Ayacucho,[5] attempted a military conquest of Cuzco.[6] In response to the impending invasion, Viracocha Inca fled Cuzco and Inca Yupanqui, a younger son of Viracocha Inca, usurped political authority from his father and the appointed heir.[7] Inca Yupanqui appealed to the various ethnic groups of the Cuzco region for help, temporarily uniting the Cuzco area, and attacked the advancing Chanca forces. It is said that the Chanca were defeated in a battle where even the large stones of the Cuzco area were transformed into warriors to fight alongside the young Inca. The chronicles claim that Inca Yupanqui took the name Pachacuti, "Transformer of the Earth," following the Inca's surprising victory over the Chanca. The Spanish accounts also state that immediately after the Chanca war the young ruling Inca, then called Pachacuti Inca Yupanqui, implemented a massive reorganization of the Cuzco region, relocating various ethnic groups and consolidating all regional power in Cuzco. Other achievements frequently attributed to this warrior-king include rebuilding Cuzco, establishing a new religion, and creating a new calendar system.[8] It is also said that Pachacuti Inca Yupanqui, after successfully dominating the Cuzco region, began to expand his rule beyond the confines of the Cuzco region through a series of military campaigns (Betanzos [1551, Chaps. 6–10, 16] 1987; Sarmiento de Gamboa [1572, Chaps. 33–35] 1906).

The Spanish chroniclers thus interpret the development of the Inca state within a single event: the Inca victory in the Chanca war under the leadership of Pachacuti Inca Yupanqui. The sudden emergence of the Inca state from virtual chaos is set by the chroniclers within an epic context: a traditional enemy attacks, a young prince seizes authority from his aging father, and the stones that surround the city are magically transformed into warriors to aid the young prince. The narrative unfolds around the majestic actions of kings and the heroic outcomes of battles. The Inca state, according to these traditional accounts, emerged fully developed from the Chanca war, and the processes of historical and social change in the Cuzco region are set in terms of Pachacuti Inca Yupanqui's personal achievements. In the words of Brundage (1963:95), "The Chanca victory is presented to us in the sources as the most striking event in all Inca history, the year one, as it were."

This account or theory of Inca state development, first recorded by the Spanish chroniclers in the sixteenth century, continues to be widely accepted today (Rowe 1944, 1945, 1957, 1970, 1985; Dwyer 1971; Brundage 1963, 1967; Kendall 1974, 1985; Patterson 1985). For example, a traditional description of Inca state development in the Cuzco region has recently been presented by Niles:

The Chancas invaded Cuzco and posed a serious enough threat to cause Viracocha to abandon the city (Sarmiento de Gamboa cap. 27; 1960:232–234; Pachacuti 1968:296; Betanzos cap. 6; 1968:17). His son, the prince Inca Yupanqui, took charge of the defense of the city and successfully repelled the invaders. With the support of the army and the grateful residents of Cuzco, he took the throne from his father, who never returned to Cuzco (Betanzos cap. 6; 1968:19–20; Pachacuti 1968:297).

Taking the name Pachacuti, "transformer of the Earth," to commemorate his victory (Sarmiento de Gamboa cap. 27; 1960:233), the new ruler took control of the old Chanca domain and doubled the area under Inca rule. In order to punish the Chancas and consolidate his own holding, Pachacuti reorganized the army and began systematically to wage war at the peripheries of the area under Inca influence. The Inca Empire was begun. (Niles 1987:7)

Another example is presented in Rowe's classic article "Inca Culture at the Time of the Spanish Conquest":

The Chanca attack was delayed until Viracocha was an old man, perhaps with the deliberate intention of striking the *Inca* when their leadership was weak. When it came, the threat was so serious that many *Inca*, including Inca Urcon, the announced heir to the crown, believed resistance was impossible. Viracocha was persuaded that the cause was hopeless and took refuge with Inca Urcon in Caquia-Xaquixahuana, a fort above Calca, . . . Yupanqui assumed command and used every inducement to secure allies, even to bribing the *Cana* and *Canchi* to send contingents (Polo, 1917 a, p. 46). The *Chanca* invested the city and tried to take it by storm, but the *Inca* resisted heroically, and, at the critical moment, Yupanqui cried out that the very stones were turning to men to help them. The attack was repulsed, and Inca Yupanqui had the stones from the battle-field collected and placed in the city's shrines. . . . In subsequent battles, the *Chanca* were soundly defeated, and the *Inca* suddenly became the most powerful people in the Andes. (Rowe 1946:204)

These recent interpretations of the development of the Inca state are based on direct, or what can be called literal, readings of the Spanish chronicles. The research goal is the creation of an event-based historical narrative, a goal that is achieved by combining various accounts of the Chanca war and Pachacuti Inca Yupanqui's rise to power into a single account. In their analysis of the chronicles the researchers assume that the historical consciousness of the sixteenth- and seventeenth-century Spaniards or Spanish trainees who recorded the accounts, as well as that of the indigenous informants who provided the accounts to the pamphleteers, is comparable to our own. More concretely stated, the researchers assume that the information presented in the chronicles can be, and should be, read as if it were made up of historical facts.[9]

Since these researchers assume that the chronicles contain historical facts, they have attempted to reconstruct the history of the Inca by arranging the various mythological/historical events in chronological order. In this way these studies reproduce the very literary form from which their data were extracted. Many of the modern works are simply composite chronicles that attempt to record, with little analysis or interpretation, a series of events in Inca history in the order in which they are thought to have occurred. As Urton (1990:9) has pointed out, literal readings of the Spanish chronicles promote the dubious proposition that a singular and true version of Inca history exists, and they encourage "the systematic rephrasing of the many *differences* that one encounters in the various accounts in the chronicles as *discrepancies*. . . ." The end result is that much of "Andean history and historiography is about resolving discrepancies (e.g., by choosing one account over others) rather than about trying to understand and explain why and how different chroniclers . . . have arrived at fundamentally different interpretations of Inka history" (Urton 1990:9).

It is also important to note that traditional interpretations of state development in the Cuzco region concentrate on describing a limited number of events, and specific individuals are taken to be the ultimate objects of historical research (Ricoeur 1980:8; Fogelson 1989:135). For example, the reforms implemented by Pachacuti Inca Yupanqui following his victory in the Chanca war are thought to have been so profound that they not only resulted in the formation of the Inca state, but also permanently altered the fundamental structure of Andean social and political order: "The 90-odd years of the *Inca* Empire formed the most significant period in all of Andean Indian history. In it, the whole of Andean culture was given a new orientation and turned into paths of development which it is still following after four centuries of alien domination. In a very real sense, modern Indian history begins, not with the Wars of Independence or with the Spanish Conquest, but with the organizing genius of Inca Pachacuti in the 15th century" (Rowe 1946:329). Under this traditional, or what I will call event-based, view of history, Pachacuti Inca Yupanqui is promoted to the level of a culture hero and his activities are seen as the prime agent of historical change for the Inca.

It has only been in recent years that a number of scholars have become increasingly uneasy with the traditional explanation of Inca state growth as presented by the chronicles. Current scholarship in both history and anthropology suggests that, even though the Inca expansion may have occurred rapidly, researchers should look at this phenomenon as the result of diachronic transformations in Andean social institutions, rather than as resulting from the serendipitous outcome of a single battle and the aspirations of a specific individual. Various authors have, therefore, developed a number of different causal models for the development of the Inca state. For example, Rostworowski de Diez Canseco (1978, 1988) suggests that the formation of early alliances in the Cuzco region, and the initial expansion of the Inca, resulted primarily through the manipulation of institutionalized exchange relationships rather than through military conquests. Lumbreras (1978), on the other hand, emphasizes the importance of class conflict in the development of the Inca state as well as traditional hostilities between the Cuzco region and the Chanca. Murra (1972, 1980), Schaedel (1978), and Isbell (1978) have each stressed the importance of economic management and systems of redistribution in the development of the Inca state, while others have suggested that the Inca's system of inheritance was of central importance to the state's formation (Conrad 1981; Demarest and Conrad 1983; Conrad and Demarest 1984; Patterson 1985). Through the investigation of broad categories of social and economic organization these authors have attempted to shift the focus of research away from the actions of a single individual (i.e., Pachacuti Inca Yupanqui) to the study of more general processes of social change.

The accuracy of literal interpretations of the chronicles has come under increasing scrutiny over the past several decades by a separate group of anthropologists. It has long been noted that the development of the Inca state represents a very difficult subject for historical studies since the indigenous peoples of the Andes did not develop any form of written records. As a result, the only records available on this complex polity are Spanish documents written, on the basis of native testimonies, during the first generations of Spanish control in the Andes. Recent studies suggest that literal interpretations of these chronicles require the acceptance of numerous untested assumptions and do not fully take into account the prejudices of the Spaniards who wrote them. In addition, it is evident that the natives themselves also actively attempted to manipulate "historical" information in order to better their own positions (Urton 1990).

The ethnohistorical studies of Tom Zuidema (1964, 1977, 1982, 1983, 1986), Pierre Duviols (1979a, 1979b), Gary Urton (1989, 1990), and Åke

Wedin (1963) have been especially critical of literal interpretations of the events described in the Spanish chronicles. Urton summarizes their criticisms of literal interpretations of the chronicles in a brief review of Zuidema's work: ". . . because of the impossibility of evaluating the historicity of the material in the chronicles from an indigenous, pre-Hispanic point of view, we cannot use the data provided by the Spanish chronicles with any confidence to construct a history of the Inkas. Rather, the chronicles should be viewed, according to Zuidema, as containing intentional representations of the organization and structure of the Inka empire that were informed and motivated by various pre-Hispanic and colonial political, social, ritual, and other considerations by *both* the indigenous informants and the chroniclers themselves (1964, 1982, 1983c, 1986)" (Urton 1990:6). These researchers challenge the validity of literal interpretations of the chronicles as impressionistic in method and Eurocentric in their modes of interpretation. They also argue that much of the information recorded in the Spanish chronicles consists of mythical representations of the past and, as such, cannot be used in scholarly reconstructions of the pre-Hispanic periods in the Andes.

The current perspectives of Inca state development in the Cuzco region can be divided into three general groups. Some scholars follow the traditional interpretations of Inca history as presented in the Spanish chronicles (Rowe 1944, 1945, 1946, 1957, 1970, 1985; Dwyer 1971; Brundage 1963, 1967; Kendall 1974, 1985; Niles 1987). For them the state emerges as the result of a specific conflict with the Chanca and the unique and charismatic leadership of Pachacuti Inca Yupanqui. The second group of scholars examines the development of the Inca state through the interactions of broader segments of Inca society. These scholars suggest that the Inca state developed through time as the result of transformations of social, economic, and religious institutions (Murra 1972; Rostworowski de Diez Canseco 1978; Lumbreras 1978; Schaedel 1978; Isbell 1978; Conrad and Demarest 1984). Within this perspective the Chanca war may be seen as a component, if not a precipitant, of that developmental process, rather than as the direct cause of state formation. There are, however, many different views among this group and there is no general agreement on the central mechanisms or institutions involved in the process of state growth.

The third group of researchers suggests that the chronicles should not be read as direct or literal representations of the past. These researchers believe that the oral traditions that the Spaniards recorded in their chronicles are distorted by the Spanish authors and Western notions of historicity (Zuidema 1964, 1977, 1983, 1986; Duviols 1979a, 1979b), and by the self-interested representations of Inca history presented by various indigenous inhabitants (Urton 1989, 1990). These anthropologists have rejected literal interpretations of the chronicles as valid means of understanding pre-Hispanic social development in the Andes and argue in favor of developing new approaches to the study of the Andean past.

Throughout this work, it will be argued that archaeological research can and should play an important role in resolving various issues of this debate. Archaeological projects, conducted independently of information presented in the Spanish chronicles, can provide data sets that may be compared with information found in the documentary sources. Unfortunately, as noted by John Murra (1984:77) and Richard Burger (1989:56), there has been surprisingly little archaeology conducted in the Inca heartland. The general lack of systematic archaeological research in the Cuzco region has seriously constrained researchers' abilities to test various models against independent archaeological data. Conrad and Demarest write: "In theory archaeology could greatly further our understanding of the pre-imperial Inca by revealing the precise chronology of their cultural development and by serving as a means of evaluating conflicting hypotheses derived from the chronicles. The practical problem is that the archaeological data available at present are not very extensive" (1984:96).[10]

Most archaeological projects in the Cuzco region have concentrated either on conducting test excavations at single sites or on collecting surface pottery from a limited number of sites. With the possible exception of Ann Kendall's (1976) work in the Cusichaca Valley, located northwest of the immediate Cuzco region, and Kenneth Heffernan's (1989) study of the Limatambo region west of Cuzco, there have been no systematic regional surveys to investigate the subsistence-settlement systems of the Early Inca and Inca periods.[11] Without a regional perspective for the Cuzco area, the development of a model of early state formation for the Inca that is inclusive of, and supported by, archaeological evidence has not been possible. The present investigation begins to address the need for more thorough archaeological and historical research in the heartland of the Inca through a synthesis of regional survey, excavation, and historical and ethnographic data collected in the Province of Paruro (Department of Cuzco) from 1984 to 1987.

Related Research in the Inca Empire

Despite the large size and complexity of the Inca Empire, few archaeological studies have been conducted to investigate its early formation in the Cuzco region. There have been, however, a number of recent archaeological projects that have focused on the processes through which the Inca incorporated new regions into the state once it had expanded beyond the confines of the Cuzco region. A brief review of several key studies is necessary because, in the absence of a focused body of regional archaeological studies in the Cuzco region, they present the only framework through which the relations of Incas and non-Incas have been addressed archaeologically and through which the processes of Inca expansionism have been analyzed.

One of the earliest examinations of Inca state expansionism was presented by Menzel (1959). After a short review of the historical information concerning the pre-Inca and Inca occupations on the south coast of Peru, Menzel examined the Late Horizon architectural and ceramic remains in the same region. Through a comparison of the architectural remains, the settlement patterns, and the historical information for a series of coastal valleys, she concluded that there were distinct differences in the social and political organizations of the coastal valleys at the time of their conquest by the Inca. In addition, she suggested that the form and intensity of post-conquest Inca occupations varied in direct response to the form of social organization that controlled the valley prior to the arrival of the Inca:

> The Incas took advantage of existing centralization in Chincha and Ica, building their administrative centers at the focus of native authority. They probably ruled through the native nobility in both valleys. In the valleys in which there was no centralized authority already, the Incas imposed their own, constructing an administrative center at some convenient point to serve as the focus of Inca control. These administrative centers were located on the Inca coast road, a fact which emphasizes the military and administrative significance of the road system. No effort was made in this area to concentrate the population in towns, and existing patterns of settlement were not seriously interfered with. (Menzel 1959:129)

Menzel's investigation provided several important contributions to Andean archaeology and the study of the Inca state. Her work differed from many earlier studies in that her investigation synthesized historical materials and archaeological remains to examine broader issues of Inca state development and control. By doing so, she emphasized the fact that while the historical sources are a valuable aid in the interpretation of the Inca Period, archaeological research can provide its own sensitive interpretations. In the words of Morris (1988:234–235), "Menzel's work demonstrated, on the one hand, that written sources and archaeology can be effectively used together and, on the other, that archaeology in and of itself can add significantly to our understanding of the Inca."

A second important feature of Menzel's work is that it expanded the realm of Inca research far beyond the core region of the Cuzco Valley, and beyond the Cuzcocentric perspective of the chronicles. Many of the earlier archaeological studies on the Inca were limited to explorations of the Cuzco region (Bingham 1910, 1922, 1930; Fejos 1944), site descriptions (Muelle 1945; Pardo 1957), and the establishment of pottery sequences (Bingham 1915a; Valcárcel Vizquerra 1934, 1935; Pardo 1938, 1939; Rowe 1944). While the Inca heartland and the general descriptions of the Inca state provided by the Spanish chronicles represented a logical beginning point for the study of Inca culture, their selection tended to promote a distorted impression of a monolithic empire. By examining a region far from the center of Inca state development, Menzel emphasized the multiethnic character of the empire and the various strategies that the Inca state adopted while assimilating different polities into the empire.

In recent years the nature of Inca sovereignty, the means through which Inca rule was imposed on subject polities, and the process of Inca imperial consolidation of other ethnic groups have become a central research problem for a number of archaeological studies in Peru. A particularly important archaeological investigation that examined the relations between the Inca Empire and its subject polities was conducted by Morris and Thompson at the site of Huánuco Pampa in the north central highlands of Peru (Morris 1972, 1974, 1982; Morris and Thompson 1985). The Inca center of Huánuco Pampa contains more than 4,000 structures and is situated, not in a productive maize zone, as might be expected of an Inca regional center, but in a relatively high (3,800 masl) and remote location. Morris produced a series of studies that examine the maintenance of this large Inca center and the process of consolidation that occurred around it. Concentrating on its large system of nearly 500 storage houses and on excavations conducted within various sections of the city itself, Morris (1967, 1982:155) studied the means through which this provincial center acted as an intermediary between the ruling elite in Cuzco and the indigenous peoples of the region. While investigating the processes of Andean statecraft, Morris concluded that one of the primary roles of Inca regional centers, such as Huánuco Pampa, was the collection and redistribution of goods. Building on the influential work of ethnohistorian John Murra (1962, 1968, 1972, 1980), Morris also suggested that the Inca attempted to legitimatize their rule through modifications of traditional Andean relations of reciprocity: ". . . the relationships between the Inca, or the state, and the people they ruled, were conditioned by a complex web of reciprocities. Most of this reciprocity involved "gifts" of cloth, and of food and of other forms of maintenance or "hospitality" on the state's site. The subjects were obliged to give of their own energies in the state's fields, armies, and its public work projects" (Morris 1978:320).

Spanish documents suggest that at least four separate ethnic groups (Chupaychu, Yacha, Wamali, and Queros) occupied the Huánuco Pampa region during Inca rule and were all directly involved in the construction and maintenance of the local Inca installations in the area (Morris and Thompson 1985; LeVine 1987). Although Morris and Thompson did not conduct a systematic regional survey, they did direct several test excavations at sites specifically mentioned in the early colonial documents for the region. These suggest that the different ethnic groups were governed indirectly through a local, but Inca-supported, ruler (Morris and Thompson 1985:164). In the Huánuco Pampa region, the Inca may have been more concerned with the construction of their support facilities and the extraction of labor from the local ethnic groups than with the rapid restructuring of the local-level socio-political organizations: "As we have seen, the architectural and ceramic remains suggest that the new level of governance was precisely that: a new level that remained separate from the existing polities of the region. The Inca policy in Huánuco appears to have emphasized the maintenance and manipulation of diversity rather than an attempt to integrate through the creation of cultural uniformity" (Morris and Thompson 1985:165). Although the construction of the large Inca site of Huánuco Pampa and the various Inca state facilities in the region required massive amounts of labor, the indigenous subsistence-settlement system appears to have remained relatively unchanged.

The effect of the Inca conquest on regional ethnic groups has also been a major theme of investigation for the Upper Mantaro Archaeological Research Project. The Upper Mantaro Valley was occupied during the late prehistoric periods by a large ethnic group known as the Wankas. Drawing on archaeological data and on a number of published *visitas* (inspections), various members of the project have concluded that the region was divided into a series of polities (Earle et al. 1980; D'Altroy 1981, 1987b; LeBlanc 1981; Hastorf 1983), the centers of which were large, nucleated villages surrounded by large defensive walls. These settlements were located in the upper agricultural production zones of the area, suggesting an emphasis on potato production. Regional archaeological surveys of the Upper Mantaro Valley show that the Inca conquest of the Wankas brought dramatic changes to the social and economic organization of the region (D'Altroy

1981:266). Major shifts in the regional subsistence-settlement systems occurred as the inhabitants of the Xauxa area were forced to abandon their fortified hilltop sites and were relocated to a series of new sites. These new sites not only were much smaller than the traditional occupations of the area but also were located in lower parts of the valley (D'Altroy 1987b:88).

As the Inca consolidated their control over the Upper Mantaro area, they built a series of installations that included the large center of Hatun Xauxa, an extensive road network, numerous storage complexes, and a series of smaller settlements. These facilities, like those established around Huánuco Pampa, represent an intensive intrusion into the preexisting social and political organization of the region and appear to have been built exclusively to meet the administrative and military needs of the empire in the region (D'Altroy 1981). At the same time, the Inca seem to have been consolidating their power in the Upper Mantaro region through the promotion of Wanka elites to act within the ranks of the state bureaucracy. D'Altroy suggests that the Inca were dependent on the pre-conquest regional Wanka organization and attempted to centralize the preexisting local administrative and production systems to their advantage: ". . . the policies enacted by the Incas in the Xauxa area seem to have been devised to expand state power by creating an independent means of production, while eliminating potential competition. The political system was centralized to mobilize manpower and goods, while interfering modestly with the economic autonomy of local groups. Conversely, the state economic system served primarily for political finance. The source of imperial support necessarily lay in the subject provinces, to whose organization the state had to adapt" (D'Altroy 1981:266).

Another perspective of imperial conquest and consolidation has been proffered by Schreiber (1987), using data from the Carahuarazo Valley. Rather than examining the processes of Inca state consolidation that occurred around large regional centers, such as Huánuco Pampa or Hatun Xauxa, Schreiber's Carahuarazo Valley case study focuses on the changes that occurred in a relatively small mountain area. In the Carahuarazo Valley, there appears to have been no major change in the pre-Inca to Inca settlement patterns: "The Inka administration of this province did not require the construction of any major administrative facility, but rather was accomplished through the imposition of a single Inka governor in a local center. In other words, the local system of administration was probably sufficiently complex to carry out the activities required by the empire, especially because no major administrative installation was needed" (Schreiber 1987:278). Nevertheless, three storage centers were built, containing a total of ninety-one Inca storehouses, and the road network in the region was improved (1987:277). These state facilities suggest that one of the Inca's central concerns in the Carahuarazo Valley was the collection and storage of surplus goods, an administrative task that could, apparently, be achieved with minimal state supervision.

Selected works of Menzel, Morris, D'Altroy, and Schreiber have been described above, since they share a common research theme: the establishment and maintenance of Inca political and economic control over ethnic groups during the expansion and consolidation of the empire. All have supplemented their archaeological data with information provided in historical documents in order to reconstruct the Inca political organization of the areas studied (Schreiber 1987:267). The conclusions drawn in these studies suggest that the Inca adopted a range of flexible policies to integrate regional ethnic groups into their empire, and the differing examples of consolidation strategies and regional diversity presented by all of these authors stand in contrast to more traditional perceptions of the Inca Empire as a monolithic polity. In the words of Franklin Pease (1982:190), ". . . Tawantinsuyu is more a complicated and extensive network of relationships than it is the apparently monolithic and showy apparatus of power that the chroniclers described in the sixteenth century." These researchers have, however, selected areas of investigation far from the Inca capital, and in doing so they have explicitly chosen to examine ethnic groups that were assimilated into the state during its later expansionistic periods. The present investigation, building on the research approach developed by these earlier works, presents a regional perspective on an earlier phenomenon: Inca state formation in the Cuzco hinterland.

The Research Problem

The processes by which provincial ethnic groups were assimilated into the developing Inca state are the subjects of this investigation. Understanding how various Cuzco ethnic groups were incorporated into the Inca state is a necessary first step in the formation of a larger explanatory model for Inca state development, independent of models suggested through analyses of late sixteenth- and early seventeenth-century Spanish documents. Specifically, this investigation focuses on the social and economic organization of three circum-Cuzco ethnic groups at the time of state formation and on the changes that occurred in the Province of Paruro as a result of incipient state growth.

At the time of the Spanish conquest, the Province of Paruro, located directly south of the Cuzco Valley, was occupied by at least three distinct ethnic groups: the Masca, the Chillque, and the Tambo (Garcilaso de la Vega [1609, Bk. 1, Chap. 20] 1945:50–51). These three ethnic groups, like others inhabiting the Cuzco region, were awarded the status of *Inca de Privilegio* (Inca of Privilege) by the Inca. Non-noble Incas by birth and occupants of lands immediately outside of the Cuzco Valley, the Inca de Privilegio were tribute-paying subjects and lower-level citizens of the Inca state (Guamán Poma de Ayala [1615:84–85] 1980:66). The incorporation of these surplus-producing hinterland populations into a Cuzco-based polity marked the formation of a complex, regional, social hierarchy with a ruling elite, and the development of a centralized authority in the region.

A regional archaeological survey conducted in the Province of Paruro has generated data concerning settlement and artifact distribution patterns, the exploitation of resource zones, and the presence of Inca facilities during the period of state development. Test excavations conducted in the region support, complement, and extend the survey data by providing concise information for specific sites and by dating regional ceramic styles. The analysis is further strengthened by incorporating historical and ethnographic information on the social and economic organization of different ethnic groups within the core region of state development.

To evaluate the impact that incipient state formation had on the Masca, Chillque, and Tambo, and to define the changes that occurred in the Province of Paruro during the assimilation of these ethnic groups into the Inca state, this study focuses on four interrelated research problems: (1) regional relations and interactions during the Killke Period as deduced from the distribution of ceramic styles, (2) the subsistence-settlement systems before and after state formation, (3) the role of Inca facilities in the Province of Paruro, and (4) changes in the social organization of the regional ethnic groups as a result of state growth. This body of evidence is both cogent and indispensable for an understanding of the early formation of the Inca state, since it provides an opportunity to study the means through which the Inca consolidated and controlled their productive hinterlands. In addition, this investigation makes it possible to compare the predictions set forth in the traditional theory of state development and those of more processually oriented studies against a coherent body of archaeological data from the Cuzco region.

The book is divided into nine chapters. As described in this introductory chapter, the work examines the development of the Inca state in the Cuzco region during the later periods of prehistory. However, on a different level, the work critically assesses the historicity of information provided in the Spanish chronicles and compares contrasting approaches to the study of the past.

The second chapter of this book provides a general description of the social organization of the Cuzco region during the Inca Period. The chapter begins with a discussion of the regional *suyus* (geopolitical units) that formed the major territorial divisions in the Cuzco area. It also includes a brief description of the various circum-Cuzco ethnic groups that were awarded the honorary title of Inca de Privilegio. As will be discussed, the manner in which these groups became incorporated into the developing Inca state is critical to the study. Chapter 2 concludes with an examination of the principal territories controlled by the Masca, Chillque, and Tambo of the Province of Paruro, where the archaeological investigations presented in this work took place.

The third chapter describes the chronology used in the course of the investigation. It is argued that an independent chronology for the Cuzco region is needed since the dynastic succession dates provided by the chronicler Cabello Balboa can be seriously questioned and Rowe's master ceramic sequence is of limited use in the Cuzco region when examining issues of state formation.

Chapter 4 is divided into two sections. The first section discusses the modern political organization of the Province of Paruro and the environmental setting of the research area. The second section outlines and reviews the archaeological fieldwork conducted in the Province of Paruro and the research methodology applied in the province as a means to examine the economic and social organizations of the prehistoric populations.

The fifth chapter examines regional interactions and exchange relationships as reflected by ceramic distribution during the Killke Period. The first section of the chapter describes two Killke Period pottery styles found during the archaeological survey of the Province of Paruro. The second half of the chapter examines the distribution patterns of these Killke Period ceramic styles in the province and the significance these patterns hold for understanding the development of the Inca state.

Currently there is only scant information on the late prehistoric subsistence-settlement organizations of the Cuzco region. What formed the economic base of the region before the emergence of the Inca state? How did state growth affect the subsistence-settlement systems of the Inca de Privilegio who inhabited the region south of Cuzco? To what extent was the economic base of the region restructured to meet the needs of the developing state? In an effort to begin to address these questions, the changes in the subsistence-settlement systems of the Province of Paruro during the period of state formation

are addressed in Chapter 6. Through comparing the Killke Period subsistence-settlement patterns with Inca patterns, we are able to analyze
the nature and scope of the economic reorganization implemented
among the ethnic groups south of Cuzco as part of their assimilation
into the developing Inca state.

The large Inca sites of Maukallaqta and Puma Orco are described in
Chapter 7. Possible functions of the sites are explored through the examination of archaeological and historical information. The aim of
the chapter is to identify what state facilities were necessary for the
Inca to control and consolidate the regional groups contained within
their immediate hinterland.

Changes in the social organization of regional Cuzco ethnic groups
as a result of Inca state growth are examined in the eighth chapter. Using ethnographic and historical data provided by Urton (1984, 1988,
1989, 1990) and data collected during our archaeological survey work
in the region, the Pacariqtambo area is selected as a case study. This
case study suggests that the various ethnic groups that inhabited the
region south of Cuzco during the Inca Period were divided into separate, ayllu-affiliated settlements and were organized within regional
moiety systems. Using these data as a framework, the Killke Period
settlement pattern of the Pacariqtambo region is examined.

In the final chapter, the evidence presented in the work is reviewed
and the implications that these findings have for the development of a
larger explanatory model for Inca state development are addressed.
Data from immediately south of Cuzco do not support the traditional
view of state growth, but instead indicate that state formation in the
Cuzco region was more gradual than was previously thought. Rather
than reaffirming the Inca state's sudden appearance in the Cuzco Valley after the Inca's unexpected victory over the Chanca, the data suggest that the centralization of regional authority and the development
of a stratified social hierarchy in the Cuzco region may have begun
long before this mythohistorical conflict. In addition, it is maintained
that incipient state formation was not localized within the city of
Cuzco but rather incorporated the entire Cuzco region.

2.
The Social Hierarchy
of the Cuzco Region

THIS CHAPTER EXAMINES the social organization of the Cuzco region, which at once united the various ethnic groups of the area as "Incas" and yet separated them from the ruling elite in Cuzco. This analysis begins with a description of the fully developed empire, as described to the Spaniards by native informants. It provides an introduction to the ethnic groups of the Cuzco region and an overview of the social hierarchy of the region, as seen by the Cuzco elite, at the time of the European invasion. Specific issues addressed include (1) the hierarchical and spatial relationship that existed between the Inca of Royal Blood, the Inca of Cuzco, and what are called the *Inca de Privilegio* (Inca of Privilege)—the ethnic groups living within the Cuzco region but outside of the capital city—and (2) the territorial and ethnic divisions south of Cuzco. While the purpose of this chapter is to serve as a general introduction to the ethnic composition of the Cuzco region at the time of the Spanish Conquest, rather than as an exhaustive analysis of Inca social organization, special attention is given to the territorial divisions of three groups of Inca de Privilegio living south of the Cuzco Valley: the Masca, the Chillque, and the Tambo.[1] In the following chapters, I provide descriptions of the economic and social organizations of these southerly groups prior to the development of the Inca state and attempt to explicate the processes by which these groups were subsequently assimilated into the Inca state.

The Suyus of the Inca

The Inca divided their immense empire into four major geopolitical units, or *suyus*, which radiated out from the sacred capital of Cuzco. The Inca called their empire Tahuantinsuyu ("the four parts together") and named each of the four suyus after powerful ethnic groups in the respective regions. To the northwest of Cuzco lay the region of Chinchaysuyu, which encompassed the north coast and sierra of Peru and extended into Ecuador. To the northeast of Cuzco lay Antisuyu, which included the upper drainages of the Amazon River and the eastern slopes of the south central Andes. The southeastern quadrant of the Inca Empire, Collasuyu, included the Lake Titicaca region as well as northern Chile, northern Argentina, and most of modern Bolivia. The fourth suyu of the Inca Empire, Cuntisuyu, lay to the south and southwest of Cuzco and encompassed the distant regions of Arequipa and the south central coast of Peru.

The broad regional boundaries of the four great Inca suyus across the Andes and the coastal regions of South America have long been recognized, yet the exact boundaries of these suyus in the Cuzco region have only recently been identified. In 1977 Waldemar Espinoza Soriano published a report, dating to 1577 and written for Viceroy Toledo, which includes a list of villages within a 90-km circumference of Cuzco in accordance with their traditional suyu affiliation (Espinoza Soriano 1977). Zuidema and Poole (1982:85) plotted the location of these villages to estimate the boundaries of the suyus (Map 2). According to the 1577 document, the northwestern quarter of the empire, Chinchaysuyu, was the largest of the four divisions. This suyu arched from the province of Cotabamba (southwest of Cuzco) to the Valley of Calca (northeast of Cuzco). The northeastern quarter, Antisuyu, appears to have contained the northern bank of the Huatanay River near Cuzco and parts of the Vilcanota/Urubamba River from Caycay to Lamay; it extended into the Paucartambo region. Collasuyu, lying to the southeast of Cuzco, contained the upper drainage system of the Vilcanota/Urubamba River. Finally, Cuntisuyu lay to the south and southwest of Cuzco and contained the upper drainage system of the Apurimac River.

The Social Hierarchy of the Cuzco Region

The Cuzco region was inhabited by a number of semiautonomous ethnic groups that controlled contiguous territories within the regional suyu system. Detailed information concerning the ethnic groups of the region and the social relationships that bound them to the Inca of Cuzco is provided by three independent chroniclers: Felipe Guamán Poma de Ayala, Garcilaso de la Vega, and Juan de Santa Cruz Pachacuti Yamqui Salcamayhua. These three indigenous chroniclers were personally familiar with the Cuzco social hierarchy as it existed in the immediate post-conquest period. As such, they provided unusually ac-

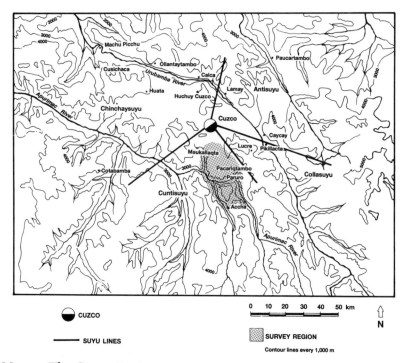

CUZCO

SUYU LINES

0 10 20 30 40 50 km

⇧
N

SURVEY REGION

Contour lines every 1,000 m

Map 2. The Cuzco Region

curate information on the spatial distribution of ethnic groups in the region (Table 1). In addition, the range and depth of information that is provided by these three chroniclers is enhanced by their differing ethnic backgrounds, which lead each of them to view the same social reality through his own perspective.

Guamán Poma de Ayala and the Social Hierarchy of the Cuzco Region

In several passages of his work *El primer nueva corónica y buen gobierno*, Guamán Poma de Ayala describes the social hierarchy of the Cuzco region and the administrative organization of the empire in terms of ranked kin groups. For the purpose of this investigation, I will concentrate on four separate, but nearly identical, lists in which he describes his vision of the social divisions that existed in the Cuzco region during Inca rule. The first of these lists is presented in Guamán Poma de Ayala's conception of the Pacariqtambo origin myth (Guamán Poma de Ayala [1615:79–85] 1980:62–66). In this account he describes how the first mythical Inca, Manco Capac, and his three broth-

Table 1. Inca de Privilegio as Described by Garcilaso de la Vega, Guamán Poma de Ayala, and Pachacuti Yamqui Salcamayhua

Garcilaso Bk. 1 Cp. 20	Garcilaso Bk. 1 Cp. 23	Guamán Poma[a] (1980:690)	Guamán Poma (1980:66)	Guamán Poma (1980:310)	Pachacuti (1950:273)	Location
Antisuyu						
1 Poques[b]	3 Poques					Paucartambo Cz.
Cuntisuyu						
2 Masca		11 Masca	4 Masca	8 Masca	3 Mascas	Paruro Cz.
3 Chillque	6 Chillqui	14 Chillque	10 Chilque	10 Chillque	4 Chillques	Paruro Cz.
4 Pap'ri		15 Papri			5 Papres	Acomayo Cz.
		12 Tanbo[c]			2 Tambos	Paruro Cz.
		13 Acos[d]	9 Acos	9 Acos		Acomayo Cz.
		16 Yana Uara	12 Yana Uara	13 Yana Uara		Tambobamba Ap.
Chinchasuyu						
5 Mayu		1 Mayu	4 Mayu	11 Mayo	7 Mayos	Anta Cz.
6 Cancu		2 Cancu			8 Tancos	Anta Cz.
7 Chinchapucyu						Anta Cz.
8 Rimactampu		7 Rimactampu				Anta Cz.
9 Y'úcay						Anta Cz.
10 Tampu[e]		6 Tanbo	5 Tanbo	2 Tanbo		Urubamba Cz.
		1 Anta	1 Anta	1 Anta		Anta Cz.
		2 Sacsa Uana	7 Equeco XaxaUana?			Anta Cz.

Table 1. (*continued*)

		3 Quilis Cachi	14 Quichiua	5 Quillis Cachi	9 Quillisscches	Anta Cz.?
		5 Quichiua	6 Lari	12 Quichiua	6 Quicchguas	Curawasi Ap.
		7 Lare	8 Uaro Conde	7 Lari		Urubamba Cz.
				6 Uaro Condo		Anta Cz.
Collasuyu						
			9 Ayamarca			Quispican. Cz.
10 Quespicancha						Quispican. Cz.
11 Muina	4 Muina					Quispican. Cz.
12 Urcos	8 Urcos					Quispican. Cz.
13 Quéhuar		8 Queuar	3 Quiuar	3 Queuar		Quispican. Cz.
14 Huáruc	5 Huáruc	9 Uaroc	2 Caca Guaroc?	4 Uaroc	1 Quiguares	Quispican. Cz.
15 Cauiña		10 Cauiña	13 Cauina	11 Cauina		Quispican. Cz.
Location unknown						
		14 Chilpaca				?

[a] In this list Guamán Poma de Ayala places several of the Inca de Privilegio in different suyus than Garcilaso de la Vega. For example, Guamán Poma de Ayala places Masca, the Tambo (of Pacariqtambo), and the Chillque in Collasuyu rather than Cuntisuyu. I have elected to follow Garcilasco de la Vega's suyu placement of these Inca de Privilegio as it conforms with information provided in other documents (Espinoza Soriano 1977; Poole 1984; Ulloa 1909; Zuidema 1983; Zuidema and Poole 1982).

[b] The numbers preceding the ethnic group names denote their order in the original texts.

[c] Pacariqtambo.

[d] According to a 1577 document Acos was located in Collasuyu (Espinoza 1977; Zuidema 1977; Zuidema and Poole 1982).

[e] Ollantaytambo.

ers and four sisters emerged from a cave called "Tanbo Toco" (Tambotoco) or "Pacaritanbo" (Pacariqtambo) and their journey to the Cuzco Valley via the mountain of "uana cauri" (Huanacauri).[2] Guamán Poma de Ayala also describes how a large number of people traveled with the royal siblings on their mythical journey to Cuzco. This entourage included representatives of the groups he calls the "uaccha" (poor) Inca of the Cuzco region, or what other chronicles have described as the Inca de Privilegio:

> Que todos los que tienen orexas se llaman *yngas*, pero no son perfe-tos, cino son yndios pobres y gente uaja ni son caualleros, cino pi-cheros. Destos dichos que tienen orexas, sólo uno fue rrey Ynga pri-mero, *Mango Capac*. Por eso le nombró *capac* [poderoso]; que dezir *ynga* es común, no es rrey, cino *capac apo* quiere dezir rrey. Y ací fue primero el *Ynga Mango Capac*, el segundo, *Anta ynga, Caca Guaroc ynga, Quiuar ynga, Masca ynga, Tanbo ynga, Lari ynga, Equeco, Xaxa Uana ynga, Uaro Conde ynga, Acos ynga, Chilque ynga, Mayo ynga, Yana Uara ynga, Cauina ynga, Quichiua ynga*. (Guamán Poma de Ayala [1615:84–85] 1980:66)

> All those who have pierced ears are called Inca, but not all are per-fect; rather some are poor Indians and low people who are not gentlemen, but tribute payers. Of those mentioned who have pierced ears, only one was the first Inca king, Manco Capac. Be-cause of this they called him *capac* (royal); that is, Inca is common, it is not king, but *capac apu* means king, and so the first Inca was Manco Capac, the second Anta Inca, Caca Guaroc Inca, Quiuar Inca, Masca Inca, Tambo Inca, Lari Inca, Equeco, Xaxa Uana Inca, Uaro Conde Inca, Acos Inca, Chillque Inca, Mayo Inca, Yana Uara Inca, Cauina Inca, Quichiua Inca.

In this description Guamán Poma de Ayala takes care to explain that although Manco Capac and his royal siblings traveled with other groups, there was, nevertheless, a clear hierarchical order among them.

The "poor Inca" (or the Inca de Privilegio) described by Guamán Poma de Ayala as living in the Cuzco hinterland formed the lower class of producers who supported the ruling elite of the capital through their tribute. Guamán Poma de Ayala specifically describes the subservient position and image of the Inca de Privilegio in compar-ison to the ruling Cuzco elite:

> En la ley de los *Yngas* se ordenaua para ser rrey, *Capac Apo Ynga. Ynga* no quiere dezir dezir [sic] rrey cino que *ynga* ay gente uaja

como *Chilque ynga* ollero; *Acos ynga* enbustero; *Uaroc ynga Llulla Uaroc* mentiroso; *Mayo ynga* falzo testimoniero; *Quillis Cachi, Equeco ynga* lleua chismes y mentiras; *poquis colla millma rinre;* estos son *yngas.* Y ací no es señor ni rrey ni duque ni conde ni marqués ni caualleros *yngas* cino son gente uaja *ynga* y pecheros. (Guamán Poma de Ayala [1615:117–118] 1980:96)

In the law of the Inca they ordained "Capac Apu Inca" to be king. Inca does not mean king. Instead as Inca there are low-status people like Chillque Inca potter; Acos Inca cheater; Uaroc Inca Llulla Uaroc liar; Mayo Inca false witness; Quillis Cachi, Equeco Inca bearers of jokes and lies; Poquis Colla *millma rinre* (term unknown). These are Inca. Therefore they are neither lord nor king nor duke nor count nor marquis nor gentlemen Inca, but they are common Inca people and tribute payers.

According to Guamán Poma de Ayala, these low-status, tribute-paying Inca of the territories surrounding Cuzco were "Inca" by virtue of two salient features. First, ancestral representatives of these ethnic groups accompanied Manco Capac on his mythical journey from the royal origin place of Tambotoco to Cuzco. Second, various ethnic groups of the Cuzco region, like the Inca of Cuzco and the imperial ruler himself, wore earspools. The custom of the Inca wearing earspools and the journey of Manco Capac from Tambotoco to Cuzco are intimately related. The *huaca* (shrine) of Huanacauri is said to represent one of the brothers of Manco Capac who was turned to stone during the journey to Cuzco, and it was the shrine of Huanacauri which, according to Inca mythology, introduced the custom of ear piercing to the Inca.[3]

In a later section of his *Primer nueva corónica*, Guamán Poma de Ayala, a native of the Huánuco region, presents another list of Cuzco ethnic groups very similar to the two outlined above. In this passage, he suggests that the Cuzco ethnic groups were classified as Inca by the people living outside of the Cuzco region, and he stresses the symbolic linkage between Inca ear perforations and their hierarchical status:

Cómo tenía sus uicios y horadamientos y costumbres antigos de los *Yngas Capac Apo Ynga* y de los otros *yngas auguiconas* y comunes *yngas,* Hanan Cuzco, Lurin Cuzco, *Anta ynga, Tanbo ynga, Queuar ynga, Uaroc ynga, Quillis Cachi ynga, Uaro Condo ynga, Lari ynga, Masca ynga, Acos ynga, Chillque ynga, Cauina ynga, Quichiua ynga, Yana Uara ynga, Chilpaca* Yunga, Uro Collo, *puquis colla, milma rinri.* Cada uno conforme a su calidad se ahora-

dauan las orexas en su ley y serimonia que usuaron en tiempo del
Ynga. (Guamán Poma de Ayala [1615:337] 1980:310)

As they had their courts, ear perforations, and ancient customs of
the Inca *Capac Apu Inca* (Royal Lord Inca) and other *Auquiconas*
(noble) Incas and Inca commoners: Hanan Cuzco, Hurin Cuzco,
Anta Inca, Tanbo Inca, Queuar Inca, Uaroc Inca, Quillis Cachi
Inca, Uaro Condo Inca, Lari Inca, Masca Inca, Acos Inca, Chillque
Inca, Cauina Inca, Quichiua Inca, Yana Uara Inca, Chilpaca Yunga,
Uro Collo, Puquis Colla, *milma rinri* (term unknown). Each one of
them, according to his rank, pierced his ears according to the law
and ceremony which they used in the time of the Inca.

The social hierarchy of the various ethnic groups in the Cuzco region is emphasized in the above quote. Of paramount importance in
the social hierarchy of the imperial capital, according to Guamán
Poma de Ayala, were the royal and noble Inca by birth, the Capac Apu
Inca and auquiconas, respectively. Below them were the people of
Hanan (Upper) and *Hurin* (Lower) Cuzco, who held a variety of different privileges and obligations to the Inca state. Below the Inca of
Hanan and Hurin Cuzco, on the lowest level of the regional social hierarchy, were the ethnic groups living outside the Cuzco Valley.

Later in his chronicle, Guamán Poma de Ayala presents a fourth description of the social hierarchy in the Cuzco area within a model of
Inca kinship.[4] In this description, he expands on the social divisions
that he presented earlier, stating that the *auqui capac churi* (powerful
royal children) were the "princes" of the kingdom. These included the
sons, grandsons, and great-grandsons of the ruling Inca. Below this social stratum were the *Incacunas* (Inca people), who included the high-
status individuals of Hanan and Hurin Cuzco who were symbolically
called the great-great-grandchildren and cousins of the Inca. The lowest stratum was composed of a large number of Inca who Guamán
Poma de Ayala calls *haua* (outside) or *uaccha* (poor) Inca, and who
lived in regions surrounding the city of Cuzco. They are listed by
Guamán Poma de Ayala in relation to the four great suyu divisions
that surrounded the imperial capital:

Auqui capac churi, principes deste rreyno, hijos y nietos y bisnietos
de los rreys *Yngas* destos rreynos: don Melchor Carlos *Paullo Topa
Ynga*, don Cristóbal *Suna*, don Juan *Ninancuro*, don Felipe *Cari
Topa* . . . son casta y generación y sangre rreal deste rreyno.

Ingaconas señores caualleros *Hanan Cuzco, Lurin Cuzco Yngas*,
tartarnietos y sobrinos y sobrinas, *ñustas*, prensesas: Casta rreal
deste rreyno.

Haua ynga, Uaccha ynga, Chinchay Suyo ynga, Anta ynga, Sacsa Uana ynga, Quillis Cachi ynga, Mayu ynga, Quichiua ynga, y sus mugeres, *palla, aui:* Son yndios tributarios.

Anti Suyo ynga, Tanbo ynga, Lare ynga y sus mugeres, *palla, aui:* Son yndios tributarios

Colla Suyo ynga, Queuar ynga, Uaroc ynga, Cauina ynga, Masca ynga, Tanbo ynga, Acos ynga, Chillque ynga, Papri ynga y sus mugeres, *palla, aui:* Son yndios tributarios.

Conde Suyo ynga, Yana Uara ynga y sus mugeres se llaman *ynaca aui* y son yndios tributarios. (Guamán Poma de Ayala [1615:740 (754)] 1980:690)

Auqui capac churi, princes of this kingdom, sons and grandsons and great-grandsons of the Inca kings of these kingdoms, Don Melchor Carlos Paullo Topa Ynca, Don Cristóbal Suna, Don Juan Ninancuro, Don Felipe Cari Topa . . . are caste and generation and royal blood of this kingdom.

Incacunas gentlemen lords Hanan Cuzco, Hurin Cuzco Incas, great-great-grandsons and cousins, *ñustas*, princesses royal caste of this kingdom.

Haua Inca, uaccha Inca, Chinchay Suyo Inca, Anta Inca, Sacsa Uana Inca, Quilis Cachi Inca, Mayu Inca, Quichiua Inca, and their wives, *palla* (noble women), *aui* (common women), are tribute-paying Indians.

Anti Suyo Inca, Tanbo Inca, Lare Inca and their wives, palla, aui, are tribute-paying Indians.

Colla Suyo Inca, Queuar Inca, Uaroc Inca, Cauina Inca, Masca Inca, Tambo Inca, Acos Inca, Chillque Inca, Papri Inca, and their wives, palla, aui, are tribute-paying Indians.[5]

Conde Suyo Inca, Yana Uara Inca, and their wives they call *ynaca aui* and are tribute-paying Indians.

These four discussions by Guamán Poma de Ayala stress different essential aspects of the Inca social hierarchy. The first discussion, set in the context of the Pacariqtambo origin myth, suggests that the social hierarchy of the Cuzco region was determined in a distant time, when the mythical Manco Capac emerged from the cave of Tambotoco and journeyed to Cuzco. The ethnic groups of the Cuzco region followed Manco Capac. As such, the hierarchical social order for the Cuzco region is presented as both divinely sanctified and unchangeable, since the events that determined the various social ranks took place in a primordial setting and involved the operation of powers outside the normal realm of human experience. The second passage describes the subservient, tribute-paying status that the Inca de Privilegio held in relation to the royal inhabitants in Cuzco. The third discussion, which focuses on the earspools of the Inca, emphasizes the importance of symbolic emblems in the representation of Inca cultural identity as well as the physically distinguished internal ranks in that same identity. The origin of the earspools, like the social hierarchy of the region, is linked to the Pacariqtambo origin myth and the migration of the first, mythical Inca to the Cuzco Valley. The fourth discussion depicts the social hierarchy of the Cuzco region in terms of a descent system. This system begins with the ruling monarch, symbolically located in the center of Cuzco, and radiates from the imperial capital into the four suyus of the Cuzco region. The ethnic groups located in the hinterland of the Inca, farthest from the sacred capital, were given the ambiguous title by Guamán Poma de Ayala of "poor" or "outside" Inca.

Garcilaso de la Vega and the Social Hierarchy of the Cuzco Region

Garcilaso de la Vega also presents a detailed description of the social hierarchy of the Cuzco region and lists the major ethnic groups of the area in the first book of his *Los comentarios reales de los Incas*. Like Guamán Poma de Ayala, Garcilaso de la Vega associates the social structure of the Cuzco region with the mythical acts of Manco Capac. However, this Cuzco-born chronicler presents a different version of the Pacariqtambo origin myth and the founding of the imperial city of Cuzco from that of the chronicler from Huánuco. In Garcilaso de la Vega's version, Manco Capac and his sister/wife leave Lake Titicaca and travel to Pacariqtambo. From Pacariqtambo they walk to the mountain of Huanacauri and then descend into the Cuzco Valley. After founding the city and organizing its inhabitants, Manco Capac walks through the four suyus of the Cuzco region organizing the ethnic groups, who are later called Inca de Privilegio:

> Y es assí que al oriente de la ciudad, de la gente que por aquella vanda [Manco Cápac] atraxo, en el espacio que hay hasta el río llamado Paucartampu, mandó poblar, a una y a otra vanda del camino real de Antisuyu, treze pueblos, y no los nombramos por escusar prolixidad: casi todos o todos son de la nascíon llamada Poques. Al poniente de la ciudad, en espacio de ocho leguas de largo y nueve o diez de ancho, mandó poblar treinta pueblos que se derraman a una mano y otra del camino real de Cuntisuyu. Fueron estos pueblos de tres nasciones de diferentes apellidos, conviene a saber: Masca,

Chillque, Pap'ri. Al norte de la ciudad se poblaron veinte pueblos, de cuatro apellidos, que son: Mayu, Cancu, Chinchapucyu, Rimactampu. . . . El pueblo más alexado destos está a siete leguas de la ciudad, y los demás se derraman a una mano y a otra del camino real de Chinchasuyu. Al mediodía de la ciudad se poblaron treinta y ocho o cuarenta pueblos, los diez y ocho de la nasción Ayarmaca, los cuales se derramavan a una mano y a otra del camino real de Collasuyu por espacio de tres leguas de largo, empecando del paraje de las Salinas, que están una legua pequeña de la ciudad. . . . Los demás pueblos son de gentes de cinco o seis apellidos, que son: Quespicancha, Muina, Urcos, Quéhuar, Huáruc, Cauiña. . . .

. . . Ahora, en nuestros tiempos, de poco más de veinte años a esta parte, aquellos pueblos que el Inca Manco Cápac mandó poblar, y casi todo los demás que en el Perú havía, no están en sus sitios antiguos, sino en otros muy diferentes, porque un visorrey, como se dirá en su lugar, los hizo reduzir a pueblos grandes, juntando cinco y seis en uno y siete y ocho en otro, y más y menos, como acertavan a ser los poblezuelos que se reduzían. . . . (Garcilaso de la Vega [1609, Bk. 1, Chap. 20] 1945:50-51)

Thus to the east of the city, with the people he [Manco Capac] brought from that direction, in the region that stretches to the side of the river called Paucartampu, he ordered thirteen towns to be settled on either side of the royal road of Antisuyu. We omit their names to avoid prolixity; they are all or almost all of the tribe called Poques. To the west of the city, in an area eight leagues long by nine or ten broad, he ordered thirty towns to be established scattered on either side of the royal road of Cuntisuyu. These were peoples of three tribes with different names: Masca, Chillqui, and Pap'ri. To the north of the city he settled twenty towns with four names: Mayu, Cancu, Chinchapucyu, Rimactampu. . . . The remotest of these towns is seven leagues from the city, and the rest are scattered on both sides of the royal road of Chinchasuyu. South of the city thirty-eight to forty towns were set up, eighteen of the Ayamarca tribe, which are scattered on both sides of the royal road of Collasuyu for a distance of three leagues beginning from the place called Las Salinas, a short league from the city. . . . The remaining towns are of people with five or six names: Quespicancha, Muina, Urcos, Quéhuar, Huáruc, Caviña. . . .

Now in our own times, during the last twenty years or so, the villages founded by the Inca Manco Capac and almost all the others in Peru are not in their ancient sites, but in completely different ones, because one of the viceroys, as we shall relate in its place, had them reduced to large towns, bringing together five or six at one place and seven or eight in another, the number varying according to the size of the villages that were concentrated. . . . (Garcilaso de la Vega 1966:52–53)

Garcilaso de la Vega's version of the Pacariqtambo origin myth and the founding of Cuzco implies that the Inca de Privilegio were non-noble, indigenous occupants of the region. Garcilaso de la Vega does not suggest, as does Guamán Poma de Ayala, that the Inca de Privilegio originated with Manco Capac at Pacariqtambo and traveled with him to Cuzco. Instead, Garcilaso de la Vega's depiction asserts that the Inca de Privilegio were genealogically and geographically outsiders to Cuzco and at the same time were subservient to it.

Garcilaso de la Vega describes a hierarchy of genealogy and of space that mythically determines the social divisions in the Cuzco region. According to Garcilaso, Manco Capac traveled from Lake Titicaca to Cuzco via Pacariqtambo. The descendants of this mythical founder became the Inca of Royal Blood, while the descendants of the inhabitants of Cuzco became the Incacuna of Hanan and Hurin Cuzco. Manco Capac then recognized the ethnic groups of the Cuzco region. According to Garcilaso de la Vega's mythology, these groups were not present at the founding of the imperial capital and could not be called Inca.

Later in his chronicle, Garcilaso de la Vega describes how Manco Capac gradually began to give privileges to the inhabitants of Cuzco and the surrounding region. The first privilege awarded to these loyal subjects was the right to wear certain clothes. The second was the right to have their hair cut short, like the Inca of Royal Blood. The third, and apparently the most important, was the privilege of piercing their ears and wearing earspools:

Mas también fué con limitación del tamaño del horado de la oreja, que no llegasse a la mitad de como los traía el Inca sino de medio atrás, y que truxessen coasa diferentes por orejeras, según la diferencia de los apellidos y provincias. A unos dió que truxessen por divisa un palillo del gruesso del dedo merguerite, como fué a la nación llamada Mayu y Cancu. A otros mandó que truxessen una vedijita de lana blanca, que por una parte y otra de la oreja assomasse tanto como la cabeca del dedo pulgar; y éstos fueron la nación llamada Poques. A las nasciones Muina, Huáruc, Chillqui mandó que truxessen orejeras hechas del junco común que los indios llaman *tutura*. A la nación Rimactampu y a sus circunvezinas mandó que las truxessen de un palo que en las islas de Barlovento llaman *maguey* y

en la lengua general del Perú se llama *chuchau,* que, quitada la cor-
teza, el meollo es fofo, blando y muy livinao. A los tres apellidos,
Urcos, Y'úcay, Tampu, que todas son el río abaxo de Y'úcay, mandó
por particular favor y merced que truxessen las orejas más abiertas
que todas las otras nasciones, mas que no llegassen a la mitad del tamaño que el Inca las traía, para lo cual les dió medida del tamaño
del horado como lo havía hecho a todos los demás apellidos, para
que no eccediessen en el grandor de los horados. (Garcilaso de la
Vega [1609, Bk. 1, Chap. 23] 1945:55)

There was however, a limitation as to the size of the hole, which
was to be less than half that of the Inca's and they were to wear different objects as ear-plugs according to their various names and
provinces. Some were given as a token a splinter of wood as thick as
the little finger, as were the tribe called Mayu and Cancu. Others
were to have a little tuft of white wool which stuck out of the ear
on both sides the length of the top of the thumb; these were of the
tribe called Poques. The Muina, Huáruc, and Chillqui tribes were to
have earplugs of the common reed the Indians called *tutura.* The
Rimactampu tribe and their neighbors had them made of a plant
called *maguey* in the Windward Islands and *chuchau* in the general
tongue of Peru. When the bark is removed, the pitch is quite light,
soft, and spongy. The three tribes bearing the name Urcos, Y'úcay,
and Tampu, all dwelling down the river Y'úcay, were given special
privilege and favor of wearing larger holes in their ears than the rest,
though they were still to be less than half as large as those of the
Inca. (Garcilaso de la Vega 1966:56–57)

In this description, Garcilaso de la Vega supports Guamán Poma de
Ayala's observations that the hierarchical ranking of various ethnic
groups of the Cuzco region was determined by their genealogical and
spatial relationship to the Cuzco elite. Nevertheless, the ascribed social status of the various ethnic groups in the Cuzco region appears to
have differed with the perspective of the observer. Guamán Poma de
Ayala (1980:66, 117–118, 310, 690), born in the Huánuco region, is very
specific in his description of the ethnic groups that surrounded the
Cuzco Valley as Inca. On the other hand, Garcilaso de la Vega, the
great-grandson of the last undisputed Inca ruler Huayna Capac, saw
the Inca de Privilegio as outsiders to Cuzco. Garcilaso de la Vega
([1609, Bk. 1, Chap. 23] 1966:58), as an "Inca of Royal Blood," perceived
the Inca de Privilegio as non-Inca who were given special privileges
and a minor ceremonial status only because of their proximity to the
imperial capital.

Pachacuti Yamqui Salcamayhua and the
Social Hierarchy of the Cuzco Region

A third possible description of the social order for the Cuzco region is briefly presented by the indigenous chronicler Juan de Santa Cruz Pachacuti Yamqui Salcamayhua, as he describes the departure of Atahualpa from Cuzco (see also Zuidema 1977:278). In this chronicle, the inhabitants of the Cuzco region, loyal to the Cuzco-born Atahualpa in the civil war against his half-brother Huascar, are portrayed as leaving the capital in specific ranks, which may have served as symbolic expressions of their social order. Pachacuti Yamqui Salcamayhua writes:

> Y assi parte del Cuzco, lleuandole en su compañia á todos los *apocuracas* y *auquiconas* por su soldado, y por alabarderos de su persona, á todos los orejones de *mancopchurincuzco*, que son caballeros, y *acacacuzcos* y *aylloncuzcos*, que son caballeros particulares; y por delanteros trae á los Quiguares & Collasuyos, y Tambos, Mascas, Chillques, Papres, y Quicchguas, Mayos Tancos, Quilliscches, y por alabarderos destos trae á los Chachapoyas y Cañares en lugar de ybanguardia ó retaguardia, todos con buena horden. (Pachacuti Yamqui Salcamayhua [1613] 1950:273)

> And in this way Atahualpa leaves Cuzco, taking with him in his company all the *apocuracas* (Lord Chiefs) and *auquiconas* (nobles) for his soldiers and as personal guards, all the pierced ear people of *mancopchurincuzco* (Cuzco sons of Manco Capac), who are gentlemen, and *acacacuzcos* (term unknown)[6] and *aylloncuzcos* (Cuzco ayllus), who are special gentlemen; and as front runners he brings the Quiguares and Collasuyos, and Tambo, Masca, Chillque, Papres, and Quicchguas, Mayos, Tancos, Quilliscches, and as personal guards he brings the Chachapoyas and Cañares in the position of vanguard or rear guard, all in good order.

Although the terminology is slightly different, the relative order and composition of the social categories presented by Pachacuti Yamqui Salcamayhua are consistent with those presented in the other indigenous chronicles. Like Guamán Poma de Ayala and Garcilaso de la Vega, Pachacuti Yamqui Salcamayhua places the Inca of Royal Blood first, the nobles of Cuzco second, the citizens of Cuzco third, and the Inca de Privilegio fourth (Figure 1).[7]

Having reviewed the social stratification for the Cuzco region and the hierarchical relationships that the Inca de Privilegio held with the

Figure 1. The Social Hierarchy of the Cuzco Region (adapted from Zuidema 1986:35)

citizens of Cuzco and the ruling Inca, I will now turn to a brief examination of the Province of Paruro and the Inca de Privilegio who inhabited the region immediately south of Cuzco.

The Province of Paruro and Inca de Privilegio

Until the late 1700s, the region directly south of Cuzco was called *El Partido del Chillques y Mascas* (the Division of the Chillque and Masca). The name was drawn from the two largest ethnic groups living in the area (Figure 2). After an in-depth study of records from the conquest and early colonial periods for the Province of Paruro, Poole (1984) outlined the regions controlled by the separate groups of Inca de Privilegio south of Cuzco at the time of the Spanish invasion. The Chillque were associated with the area located between the towns of Paruro and Accha (Poole 1984:94). The territory south of the Apurimac River, especially the village of Araypallpa, appears to have been of notable importance to the Chillque. Today this village is still known by the local inhabitants as the capital of the Chillque, a claim supported by colonial documents (Poole 1984).

References to the Masca are less common than references to the Chillque in the Spanish chronicles. Nevertheless, from colonial documents it is clear that the Masca were Inca de Privilegio and that they

Figure 2. Division of the Chillque and Masca South of Cuzco (El Partido de Chilques y Masca: Partido de Paruro en 1786, Archivo General de Indias, Sevilla: Planos: Peru/Chile No. 93)

inhabited the territory between the Chillque to the south and the Inca to the north (Poole 1984:465). The northern edge of the research area, the Llaulliccasa Pass, appears to have separated the Masca from the Inca of the Cuzco Valley.

Although in her study Poole has included the inhabitants of the Pacariqtambo region within the ethnic group of the Masca, for the purposes of this work, they will be described separately under the title of the Tambo. The Tambo are presented in this investigation as a separate ethnic group, since a number of chroniclers, including Guamán Poma de Ayala, Garcilaso de la Vega, and Pachacuti Yamqui Salcamayhua, list them in their descriptions of the Inca de Privilegio.

At least four other groups of Inca de Privilegio (Quehuare, Papre, Acos, and Yanahuara) occupied various regions south of Cuzco. The Quehuares were located to the east of the Paruro River drainage system near the modern communities of San Juan de Quehuares and Rondocan. To the southeast of the Paruro drainage, across the Apurimac River, lies the region of the Papre near the communities of Pirque, Papre, Sanka, and Curma. Farther to the south, well inside the District of Acomayo, were the Acos. To the southwest of the study region, across the Velille River, were the Yanahuara (Poole 1984:84, 457–468).

As our archaeological survey did not enter into their separate territories, these groups will not be discussed in detail in this study.

Summary

Although the details of the three classificatory systems described by Guamán Poma de Ayala, Garcilaso de la Vega, and Pachacuti Yamqui Salcamayhua may vary in detail, it is important to note that the categories of hierarchically ranked genealogical sets that result from these chronicles are nearly identical. Of utmost importance in these classificatory systems is the Royal Inca and his divine ancestors in Cuzco. The lowest tier of the Cuzco social hierarchy is held by the Inca de Privilegio, who are genealogically and geographically distant from the emperor and the capital. Thus, while the system is grounded in genealogy, the actual territorial relationships that existed between the various hierarchically ranked groups reaffirm the prevailing Cuzcocentric social hierarchy. The social hierarchy of the Cuzco region is also legitimated through references to the mythical actions of Manco Capac, who is said to have established the regional ranking during a primordial setting of human existence.

Among the tribute-paying Inca de Privilegio of the state hinterland were the Masca, Chillque, and Tambo of the modern-day Province of Paruro, which were relatively small ethnic groups that occupied the region south of the capital. Unlike the dense populations of the Urubamba River Valley, who Garcilaso de la Vega claims were awarded a special ranking among the Inca de Privilegio, these southern ethnic groups held a relatively low social status with respect to Cuzco. The low status of the Masca, Chillque, and Tambo is in many ways surprising since, as will be discussed in later chapters, the region south of Cuzco contains the site of Pacariqtambo, the sacred place where the Inca believed that their ancestor, Manco Capac, emerged from the earth (Muelle 1945; Pardo 1946, 1957; Urton 1989, 1990; Bauer 1988, 1991).

This chapter has briefly presented the social organization of the Cuzco region as it was described to the Spaniards by native informants after the conquest. It serves as an introduction to the ethnic composition of the Cuzco region as well as to the hierarchical and spatial relationships that existed between the various ethnic groups of the area during the Inca Period from the point of view of the Cuzco elite. In the next chapter, the prehistoric chronology of the Cuzco region will be discussed. In succeeding chapters the focus of research will be narrowed from the social hierarchy of the Inca and the chronology of the Cuzco region in general to recent archaeological research carried out in the territories of the Masca, Chillque, and Tambo and the changes that occurred in these territories during the period of incipient state formation.

3.
The Cuzco Chronology

THROUGHOUT THIS WORK a number of interrelated terms are used to divide the late prehistoric period of Peru into sequential temporal units. These include Middle Horizon, Late Intermediate Period, and Late Horizon, as well as Huari Period, Killke Period, and Inca Period. Definitions and explanations of these terms are necessary before analyses of any archaeological data may begin.

An Introduction to the Cuzco Chronology

There is but one absolute date for the Inca Empire and that is November 16, 1532. On this date, in the Andean city of Cajamarca, the invading Spanish forces of Francisco Pizarro captured the Inca Atahualpa. The seizure of Emperor Atahualpa, and his subsequent ransom payments and death by garroting, marked the end of the indigenous rule of Tahuantinsuyu.[1] We have eyewitness accounts of the invasion of Peru by the Spaniards and chronicles of the events that occurred after their arrival; however, establishing the dates of events that took place before the arrival of the Spaniards is difficult. The task is especially challenging since the Inca did not systematically record the passing of years. According to Bernabé Cobo, a priest who spent the majority of his adult life in Peru:

> Porque ni contaban por años sus edades ni la duración de sus hechos, ni tenían algún tiempo de punto señalado para medir por él los sucesos, como contamos nosotros desde el Nacimiento de Nuestro Señor Jesucristo, ni jamás hubo indio, ni apenas se halla hoy, que sepa los años que tiene, ni menos los que han pasado desde algún memorable acaecimiento acá. Lo que suelen responder cuando se les

pregunta de cosas pasadas, como sean ya de más de cuatro o seis
años, es que aquello acaeció *ñaupapacha*, que quiere decir antigua-
mente; y la misma respuesta dan a los sucesos de veinto años atrás
que a los de ciento y de mil, salvo que cuando la cosa es muy anti-
gua, lo dan a entender con cierto tonillo y ponderación de palabras.
(Cobo [1653, Bk. 12, Chap. 37] 1956:142–143)

They did not count their age in years; neither did they measure the
duration of their acts in years; nor did they have any fixed points in
time from which to measure historical events, as we count from the
birth of our Lord Jesus Christ. Thus, there was never an Indian who
knew his age, and there are hardly any today who know how many
years old they are, much less the number of years that have elapsed
since some memorable event. When they are asked about things of
the past, if something happened more than four to six years back,
what they usually answer is that the incident occurred *ñaupapacha*,
which means "a long time ago"; and they give the same answer for
events of twenty years back as for events of a hundred or a thou-
sand years back, except that when the thing is very ancient, they express this by a certain accent and ponderation of their words. (Cobo
1979:252–253)

In light of these difficulties, John Rowe attempted, in the early
1940s, an innovative project to establish an absolute chronology for
the development and expansion of the Inca state (1944:55–59, 61; 1945).
After comparing numerous descriptions of Inca dynastic successions
found in the Spanish chronicles, Rowe (1945:275) concluded that the
succession dates provided in Cabello Balboa's work were the most
"reasonable" and "conservative." From information provided by Cabello Balboa, Rowe produced a list of dynastic succession dates for the
last five Inca rulers (Table 2). Most important, for this study, is that
Cabello Balboa's chronicle ([1586, Chap. 19] 1951:301) states that Pachacuti Inca Yupanqui usurped the throne from Viracocha Inca on the
eve of the Chanca invasion in the year A.D. 1438. This succession year
was accepted by Rowe as an accurate date and is frequently referred to
by modern scholars as the commencement year of the Inca state.[2]

However, Rowe considered the succession dates presented by Cabello Balboa for the Incas who preceded Viracocha Inca and his son
Pachacuti implausible. He writes: "Although his [Cabello Balboa's]
dates for the early Incas give impossibly long reigns, we must remem-
ber that, according to our standard version of Inca history, this period
was largely legendary and no permanent conquests had been made.
Inca history gets onto a solid footing with the reign of Viracocha, and

Table 2. *Inca Dynastic Succession (Dates Approximate)*
according to Rowe (1944, 1945) and Niles (1987)

Ruler	Reign
Manco Capac	A.D. 1250: Founding of Cuzco
Sinchi Roca	Mythical
Lloque Yupanqui	Mythical
Mayta Capac	Mythical
Capac Yupanqui	Unknown
Inca Roca	Unknown
Yahuar Huacac	Unknown
Viracocha Inca	Until A.D. 1438: Chanca War
Pachacuti Inca Yupanqui	A.D. 1438–1471
Topa Inca Yupanqui	A.D. 1471–1493
Huayna Capac	A.D. 1493–1528
Huascar Inca	A.D. 1528–1532
Atahualpa	A.D. 1533–1533

at precisely this point Cabello's dates become reasonable" (Rowe 1945:275).

Rather than using Cabello Balboa's succession dates for the eight Incas who are said to have ruled before Pachacuti, Rowe (1945:275) suggested that each Inca would have reigned for approximately twenty-five years. In this way, Rowe proposed that the founding of Cuzco by the mythical first Inca, Manco Capac, occurred at approximately A.D. 1200 (1944:57, 61; 1970:561, 562), A.D. 1250 (1945:275; 1946:199, 203; 1970:562), or A.D. 1300 (1970:562). These dates, although recognized as marking a mythical event, are widely used to date the beginning of an Early Inca Period in the Cuzco region (Rowe 1944:61, 1946:199, 1970:561, 562; Rivera Dorado 1971a:89; Alcina Franch et al. 1976:31; Morris 1988:236).

Rowe perceives the dynastic list of Inca kings presented by Cabello Balboa to be a mythical-historical continuum; the more recent Incas and events described by the chronicles are seen as historical, while the more distant personages and events are mythical. His absolute chronology for the Inca, proposed before the advent of radiocarbon dating, has served Andean studies for over four decades. There are, however, several important inconsistencies that need to be reexamined before the dates are accepted as historically accurate and usable in the analysis of Inca remains in the Cuzco region.

One of the most troubling aspects of Cabello Balboa's dates of dynastic succession is the lack of evidence to suggest that any native

South American group established a system for recording the passing of time, beyond internal divisions within a calendar year (Rowe 1945:265). As Rowe (1945:274) writes, "We will probably never be able to date the Incas exactly, for the reason that the Cuzco Indians took no interest in the passage of years." Because there is no evidence to indicate that Andean peoples developed a linear calendar, we can only suggest that Cabello Balboa's dates were not extracted from an indigenous source, but are estimates that he personally developed. The dates he suggested become even more problematic because we know little of his informants (Rowe 1945:275). In light of these observations, the presentation of Cabello Balboa's dates of dynastic succession in the current literature in terms of definitive years (i.e., 1438, 1471, 1493, 1525) lends a deceptively positive appearance to our current state of knowledge concerning the rule of the Inca and the expansion of the Inca state.

On a more interpretive level, Tom Zuidema (1964, 1982, 1983, 1986) argues that the Spanish chronicles present mythical representations of the past that cannot be read literally: "I would consider the whole of Inca history up to the time of the Spanish conquest, and even to a certain extent beyond, as mythological. Inca 'history,' then, integrated religious, calendrical, ritual and remembered facts into one ideological system, which was hierarchical in terms of space and time. This Incaic hierarchical ideology should not be confused with the Western linear conception of history imposed by the Spanish. . . . An historical chronology, up to the Spanish conquest, will have to be established independently by archaeology" (Zuidema 1982:173–174).

Pierre Duviols (1979b) has also recently argued against the historical validity of the above-mentioned dynasties and suggests, like Zuidema, that they are best viewed in relation to traditional Andean views of dual organization. Gary Urton (1990:6) has expressed similar concerns, writing, "The various accounts that are given in the chronicles concerning the Inka kings may well represent Spanish *(mis-) interpretations* of the institution of Inka kingship according to the European models of dynasties and principles of dynastic succession with which the Spaniards of the sixteenth century were very familiar."

The current chronology for the Cuzco region may, in summary, include two problematic assumptions. First, although there is currently no clear evidence to suggest that the Inca recorded the passing of years, the dates of Cabello Balboa are assumed to be from indigenous sources, rather than his own invention. Second, the current chronology assumes that the chronicles are composed of historical facts, rather than mythical representations of the past, and that an accurate timetable of Inca state growth may be established through the exaction of "reasonable" dates and the dismissal of "implausible" ones.

Within the context of 1940s archaeology, with limited research conducted in the Cuzco region and without alternative means to date the growth of the Inca state, acceptance of the dynastic succession dates presented in the chronicles, as interpreted by Rowe and others, was justified. However, the problematic assumptions included within this widely accepted Cuzco chronology underscore the need to establish a new chronology for the development of the Inca state that is independent of the sixteenth- and seventeenth-century Spanish chroniclers and thus free of the various pitfalls that literal interpretations of the chronicles can bring. With the advent of radiocarbon dating and the recent completion of a number of archaeological investigations in the Cuzco region, it is now possible to begin to develop such a chronology.

A methodological framework for an independent chronology has already been proposed by Rowe. In the 1950s and early 1960s, Rowe and his colleagues developed, through a series of excavations in the Ica Valley, a "master ceramic sequence" that divides Peruvian prehistory into a series of temporal periods based on absolute dates (Rowe 1962, 1967a). The beginning date for each period is defined by the appearance of specific ceramic types in the Ica Valley (Fig. 3, col. A). The beginning of the Middle Horizon, for example, is marked by the appearance of Huari pottery in the Ica region (ca. A.D. 550). The end of the Middle Horizon and the beginning of the next temporal division, the Late Intermediate Period, is demarcated by the appearance of a local pottery type named Ica, at around A.D. 900, in the Ica Valley sequence (Rowe 1967a). The Late Intermediate Period ends and the final epoch (the Late Horizon) of Peruvian prehistory begins with the conquest of the Ica Valley by the Inca in the latter half of the fifteenth century (ca. A.D. 1475 according to Rowe [1962:49], using information presented in the chronicles).

While Rowe's "master sequence" provides a methodological framework for developing an independent chronology of state development in the Cuzco region, it *cannot* be used directly in the area. Rowe's master sequence establishes a series of absolute dates and was not meant to be used descriptively. For example, Lunt (1987:282) writes, "the Late Intermediate Period/Late Horizon Period boundary is fixed by its Ica date [A.D. 1475], and does not shift to accommodate similar cultural events elsewhere." Thus the Late Intermediate Period/Late Horizon boundary in the Cuzco region is not contemporaneous with the Early Inca/Inca transition (see Fig. 3). According to Rowe's master sequence, the beginning of Inca state expansionism from the Cuzco Valley, which is generally thought to have taken place during the early

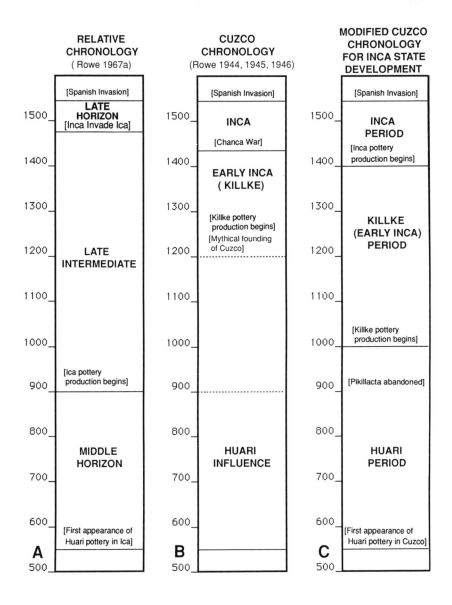

Figure 3. Chronologies of the Cuzco Region

fifteenth century, occurs well *within* the Late Intermediate Period. In addition, the Late Horizon refers to a period of time *after* the Inca expanded their control to the Ica Valley on the Pacific coast of Peru. As such, the term *Late Horizon* cannot be meaningfully used in the Cuzco setting in discussions of Inca state development, because it refers to a period of imperial expansionism that took place well after the Inca state had developed.

In the absence of better defined terminology, I will refer in this work to the era of Huari occupation in the Cuzco region (traditionally referred to as the Middle Horizon) as the Huari Period. This period is associated with the appearance of Huari pottery in the Cuzco archaeological record. I will refer to the epoch of early Inca state formation for the Cuzco region as the Killke Period, a period associated with the production of Killke and Killke-related pottery types (as defined by Rowe 1944; Dwyer 1971; Bauer and Stanish 1990). The term *Inca Period* will be used to refer to the epoch of late Inca state development and imperial expansion. This process is associated with the appearance of Inca pottery (as defined by Bingham 1915b; Eaton 1916; Valcárcel Visquerra 1934, 1935; Pardo 1938, 1939; Rowe 1944; Meyers 1975) and to a lesser extent with the appearance of Inca architectural forms (as defined by Rowe 1944; Gasparini and Margolies 1980; Kendall 1974, 1985). The tentative dates for these periods are discussed in the following section.

An Independent Chronology for Inca State Development Based on Radiocarbon Dates from the Cuzco Region

Recent archaeological work in the Cuzco region, including Dwyer's (1971) excavations in Sacsahuaman, Kendall's (1974, 1985) test excavations in the Vilcanota/Urubamba River Valley and her survey of standing stone architecture in the Cuzco region, McEwan's (1983, 1984, 1987) excavations at the Huari site of Pikillacta and the adjacent site of Choquepuquio, Hollowell's (1987, 1989) study of stone architecture in the Ollantaytambo region, and my own research in the Province of Paruro, have produced a series of radiocarbon dates. These radiocarbon dates for the Cuzco region come from two different contexts. A small number of carbon samples have been found in the course of excavations and have been used to date associated pottery. A greater number of radiocarbon dates have been obtained through samples extracted from construction materials found within the walls of prehistoric structures. Summaries of the late prehistoric radiocarbon dates recovered during excavation and from structures in the Cuzco region are presented in Tables 3 and 4, respectively.[3] These dates, although relatively few in number, provide the first opportunity to formulate

Table 3. *Radiocarbon Measurements for Late Prehistoric Periods from Excavations in the Cuzco Region*

Site	Context	Lab. No.	Radiocarbon Age		Source
			BP (Uncorrected)	*AD (Calibrated)*	
Pikillacta	Excavation/Huari	Tx 4751	1430 ± 90	541 (639) 666	McEwan 1984, 1987
Pikillacta	Excavation/Huari	Tx 4750	1350 ± 60	641 (661) 760	McEwan 1984, 1987
Tejahuasi	Excavation/Killke	B 27494	940 ± 140	980 (1037, 1142, 1149) 1250	Bauer 1990a, Chap. 5
Sacsahuaman	Excavation/Killke	GaK 2958	770 ± 140	1069 (1261) 1385	Dwyer 1971
Ancasmarca B	Excavation/Killke	1676M UCLA	660 ± 60	1278 (1284) 1390	Kendall 1974, 1985
Ancasmarca A	Excavation/Inca	930 BM	482 ± 91	1331 (1428) 1459	Kendall 1974, 1985

Table 4. Radiocarbon Measurements for Late Prehistoric Periods from Buildings in the Cuzco Region

Site	Context	Lab. no.	Radiocarbon Age BP (Uncorrected)	AD (Calibrated)	Source
Pikillacta	Wall Vine/Huari	Tx 4247	1140 ± 60	779 (892, 925, 936) 982	McEwan 1984, 1987
Pikillacta	Wall Vine/Huari	Tx 3996	1100 ± 60	885 (910, 915, 977) 996	McEwan 1984, 1987
Choquepuquio	Wall Vine/?[a]	Tx 4748	1090 ± 60	888 (979) 998	McEwan 1984, 1987
Pumamarca	Lintel/Inca?[a]	SI 6986	940 ± 40	1022 (1037, 1142, 1149) 1157	Hollowell 1987
Huchuy Cuzco	Lintel/Inca	1676G UCLA	850 ± 60	1068 (1195, 1196, 1208) 1258	Kendall 1974, 1985
Pumamarca	Lintel/Inca	SI 6987	710 ± 55	1261 (1284) 1389	Hollowell 1987
Choquepuquio	Wall Vine/?[a]	924 BM	695 ± 59	1263 (1281) 1383	Kendall 1974, 1985
Pumamarca	Lintel/Inca	SI 6988A	660 ± 50	1279 (1284) 1389	Hollowell 1987
Pumamarca	Lintel/Inca	SI 6988B	645 ± 45	1281 (1298, 1374, 1378) 1390	Hollowell 1987
Kachiqhata	Lintel/Inca	SI 6990	640 ± 55	1281 (1300, 1373, 1380) 1392	Hollowell 1987
Intihuatana	Lintel/Inca	SI 6989	515 ± 50	1332 (1417) 1434	Hollowell 1987
Canamarca	Lintel/Inca	1676D UCLA	475 ± 60	1410 (1430) 1445	Kendall 1985
Fortaleza Oll	Lintel/Inca	SI 6991A	470 ± 70	1409 (1432) 1452	Hollowell 1987
Canaraccay	Lintel/Inca	925 BM	425 ± 67	1424 (1442) 1492	Kendall 1974, 1985
Tunasmocco	Lintel/Inca	1676B UCLA	415 ± 60	1429 (1444) 1494	Kendall 1974, 1985
Fortaleza Oll	Lintel/Inca	SI 6991B	390 ± 100	1430 (1455) 1640	Hollowell 1987
Yucay	Lintel/Inca	1676K UCLA	365 ± 60	1442 (1488) 1636	Kendall 1974, 1985
Fortaleza Oll	Lintel/Inca	931 BM	295 ± 54	1495 (1534, 1536, 1638) 1653	Kendall 1974, 1985

[a]Not included in Figure 4.

an absolute chronology for the growth and development of the Inca state that is independent of the dynastic succession dates provided in the Spanish chronicles.

The beginning of the Huari Period (or Middle Horizon) in the Cuzco region is associated with the first appearance of Huari pottery. Investigations conducted by McEwan at the large Huari center of Pikillacta have provided a series of dates for the Huari occupation in the Cuzco region (McEwan 1987:42–43, 80, 89). Carbon extracted from the lowest levels of his excavations (Tx 4750 and Tx 4751) at Pikillacta indicate that the Huari presence in the Cuzco region began sometime in the mid–sixth century A.D. Samples collected from wall supports of the site (Tx 3396 and Tx 4246) suggest that a final construction phase took place around A.D. 800–850. McEwan (1987:80) concludes that the abandonment of Pikillacta would have occurred after this construction phase, "perhaps as late as 1,000 A.D."

The Killke (or Early Inca) Period for the Cuzco region, as noted above, is associated with the production of Killke and Killke-related pottery types. Currently three radiocarbon samples exist from clear Killke contexts (Table 3 and Fig. 4).[4] These include one sample from

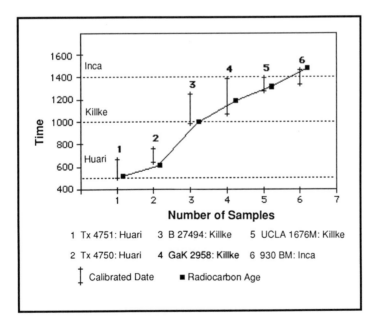

Figure 4. Radiocarbon Measurements for Late Prehistoric Periods from Excavations in the Cuzco Region

Dwyer's work at Sacsahuaman (GaK 2958), one sample from Kendall's excavations at the site of Ancasmarca (UCLA 1676 M), and one sample from my excavations at the Tejahuasi site (B 27494). These three calibrated dates and their standard deviations fall between the dates of A.D. 980 and 1390.

The Inca Period in the Cuzco region is associated with the production of Inca pottery. Only one date, however, is available from the Cuzco region from carbon found in association with Inca pottery. This date, published by Kendall (1985:347), provides a calibrated age of A.D. 1331 (1428) 1459.

Despite the small sample size and the large standard deviations presented in some of the samples, it may be tentatively concluded that the Killke Period of the Cuzco region began considerably earlier than the A.D. 1200/1250/1300 estimate currently suggested in the literature. This should not be surprising since the date was, after all, first established in 1944 to mark the *mythical* founding of Cuzco by Manco Capac. It now seems reasonable to set the approximate beginning of the Killke (Early Inca) Period in the Cuzco region around the year A.D. 1000. Furthermore, until additional work has been conducted concerning the transition between Killke and Inca pottery in the Cuzco region and until more dates are published from Killke and Inca contexts, I suggest using the year A.D. 1400 as an approximate date for the close of the Killke Period and the beginning of the Inca Period in the Cuzco region (Fig. 3, col. C).

Under the traditional model of Inca state formation, the appearance of Inca-style pottery and that of Inca-style stone architecture are assumed to have occurred simultaneously through the inspiration and supervision of Viracocha Inca and Pachacuti Inca Yupanqui. A number of radiocarbon dates that were collected from buildings within the Cuzco region by McEwan (1987:42–43, 80, 89), Kendall (1985:347), and Hollowell (1987, 1989) provide an important opportunity to examine this assumption and to develop further the Cuzco chronology (Table 4 and Fig. 5). As noted above, two of McEwan's samples from Pikillacta suggest that construction continued at this major Huari site until around A.D. 850. Currently, no radiocarbon samples have been collected from structures in the Cuzco region with clear and unquestionable associations with Killke pottery.[5] The absence of data from "Killke" structures accounts for the deficiency of dates in the A.D. 1000 and 1250 range in Table 4 and Figure 5. The one site that does provide a date in this period is Huchuy Cuzco, an Inca-style site in the Vilcanota/Urubamba River Valley, between the towns of Calca and Lamay. The surprisingly early date of a wooden lintel at the site (calibrated A.D. 1068 (1195, 1196, 1208) 1258) is interpreted by Kendall

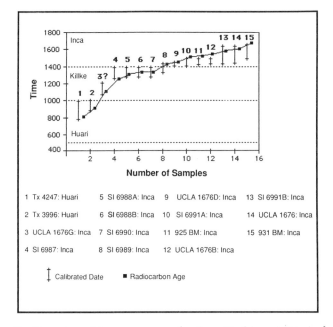

Figure 5. Radiocarbon Measurements for Late Prehistoric Periods from Buildings in the Cuzco Region

(1985:347–348) as evidence for the reutilization of older building materials by the Inca.

A series of Inca structures north of Cuzco have, however, provided a cluster of dates that fall within the thirteenth and fourteenth centuries (Hollowell 1987, samples SI 6987, SI 6988A, SI 6988B, SI 6990). These data are noteworthy because they form the earliest cluster of dates from Inca-style structures and because they come from buildings well outside the Cuzco Valley. Three structures at Pumamarca, an Inca-style site located above Ollantaytambo, provide radiocarbon dates and standard divisions between A.D. 1261 and 1390.[6] A building at the quarry of Kachiqhata, across the Urubamba River from Ollantaytambo, provides a similar age and standard deviation range of A.D. 1281 (1300, 1373, 1380) 1390. These findings suggest that Inca-style stone architecture in the region of Cuzco may have appeared for the first time between A.D. 1260 and 1390, a range of dates much earlier than previously predicted. If these dates are accurate, then some of the "Inca"-style structures in the Cuzco region may have been constructed during the Killke Period. The Ollantaytambo data highlight the need for additional research on the relationship between ceramics and architectural styles in the Cuzco region.

Five radiocarbon dates from clear Inca contexts are available from researchers working at Inca sites outside of the Cuzco region. Conrad and Webster (1989) report a date of A.D. 1580 ± 80 (calibrated A.D. 1437 (1487) 1640) from an excavated context with Inca ceramics at the site of San Antonio in the Moquegua Valley. Engel (1966) has published a radiocarbon date from a level with Cuzco-style ceramics at the site of Lurín Centinela with a date of 1465 ± 105 (calibrated A.D. 1327 (1427) 1479). Dillehay (pers. com. 1989) reports an Inca context in the Chillon Valley with a date of 1490 ± 80 (calibrated A.D. 1409 (1435) 1480). In addition, Topic and Topic (1983) provide two dates from Inca storehouses at Cerro Santa Bárbara in the Huamachuco area, 1475 ± 65 (calibrated 1409 (1430) 1447) and 1550 ± 75 (calibrated 1431 (1453) 1629).[7] All of these dates fall in the latter half of the fifteenth century and the early sixteenth century. Although many more dates are necessary before the Inca expansion can be definitively dated, these findings support many of the chroniclers who suggest that the Inca state expanded beyond the Cuzco region, and established control of an enormous Andean territory, within the span of a few generations.

To summarize, the chronology used in this investigation divides the late pre-Hispanic era in the Cuzco region into three broadly defined time periods: the Huari Period, the Killke Period, and the Inca Period (Fig. 3, col. C). Each of these periods is defined by the appearance of a specific pottery type in the archaeological record of the Cuzco region. The chronological framework relies on local ceramic types and radiocarbon dates and differs from the current Cuzco chronology, which is based on Cabello Balboa's list of dynastic successions. It also differs from Rowe's master sequence, which is based on the appearance of pottery types in the Ica Valley for the earlier periods, and on information from the chronicles for the later periods.

The following chapter will provide an introduction to the Province of Paruro. Chapter 4 also outlines and reviews recent archaeological fieldwork conducted in Paruro as well as the research methodology used during this investigation.

4.
The Research Region and Research Methodology

SINCE THE GOAL of this study is to examine the processes of Inca state development in the Cuzco region during the Killke and Inca periods, the research design includes a large archaeological survey program near the Cuzco Valley. The reliance of this investigation on archaeological survey data contrasts with previous research projects in the Cuzco region, which have generally concentrated on excavations at a limited number of Killke and Inca period sites and on generalized reconnaissance studies.[1] The research for this project was conducted in the Province of Paruro (Department of Cuzco, Peru), which lies immediately south of the Cuzco Valley (Map 3).[2] The Province of Paruro has been known since the first recorded Spanish explorations into the area as a region of exceptionally steep river valleys and limited access. The first Spanish expedition into the modern-day Province of Paruro was conducted in December of 1533 by Hernando de Soto. The expedition took place during a brief alliance between the invading Spanish forces of Francisco Pizarro and Manco Inca, as de Soto chased the Inca "general" Quisquis south of the Cuzco Valley. Quisquis and his Ecuadorian forces escaped de Soto by fleeing across the Apurimac River and burning the suspension bridge of Huajachaca behind them. De Soto and his men, unable to ford the Apurimac River, returned to Cuzco, describing the region as "the wildest and most inaccessible they had seen" (Hemming 1970:126).

The Province of Paruro

The Province of Paruro is separated from the Cuzco Valley in the north by a ridge that rises over 4,000 masl and forms the watershed between the Vilcanota/Urubamba and Apurimac rivers (Map 4). This

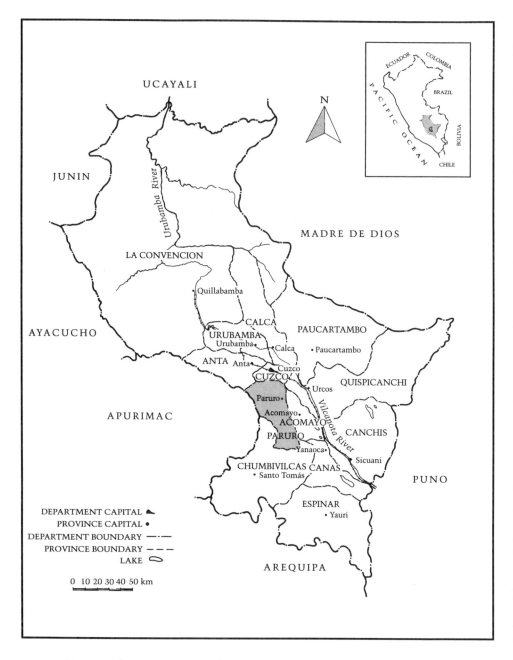

Map 3. The Department of Cuzco

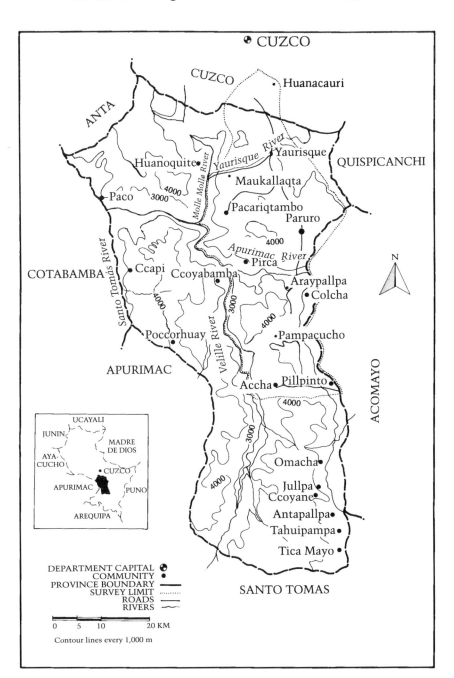

Map 4. The Province of Paruro

ridgeline is especially noteworthy because it contains the sacred mountain of Huanacauri. The southeastern and southwestern borders of the Province of Paruro are defined by the Apurimac and Santo To-más rivers, respectively. The southern boundary of the province is drawn across a high (+4,000 masl) puna region to the north of Livitaca.

The Province of Paruro is divided into nine districts: Yaurisque, Huanoquite, Pacariqtambo, and Paruro to the north of the Apurimac River and Colcha, Pillpinto, Accha, Ccapi, and Omacha to the south. The deeply entrenched Apurimac River Valley and its tributaries form the major internal political boundaries for these nine districts. The Apurimac River crosscuts the province, with one-third of the territory lying to the north and two-thirds to the south of the river. The northern third of the province is subdivided by two tributaries of the Apurimac: the Molle Molle River and the Paruro River. The Molle Molle River, which forms the boundary between the districts of Huanoquite and Pacariqtambo, enters the Apurimac River near the village of Nayhua at an elevation of 2,400 masl. The Paruro River is located east of the Molle Molle and enters the Apurimac River near the village of Cusibamba at an elevation of 2,775 masl. The Paruro River Valley is considerably wider than that of the Molle Molle River and contains the most productive agricultural land in the province.

The southern two-thirds of the Province of Paruro is divided in half by the Velille River. The isolated district of Ccapi is located to the south of the Apurimac and to the west of the Velille River. Between the Velille and the Apurimac lie the districts of Colcha, Accha, Pillpinto, and the southernmost district of Omacha. The largest town in the southern two-thirds of the province is the town of Accha.

The modern population distribution of the Province of Paruro, largely localized into the district capitals of Yaurisque, Pacariqtambo, Paruro, Colcha, Accha, Ccapi, Omacha, Huanoquite, and Pillpinto, is a direct reflection of the Spanish *reducción* (reduction) policy (Gade and Escobar Moscoso 1982). Beginning in 1571, Viceroy Francisco de Toledo implemented a systematic reorganization of the Andean demographic landscape. In an effort to more efficiently extract tribute, land, and labor as well as to provide religious indoctrination to native peoples, the Spaniards forced the local inhabitants of the Andes to abandon their traditional settlements. The rural populations of the highlands were resettled into newly created towns called *reducciones*, and the former settlements were frequently destroyed to prevent their reoccupation. Following specific Hispanic conceptions of town organization, the reducciones were built with a central plaza, a town hall, and a church. The resettlement policy of the Spaniards and the creation of large, central communities marked the end of indigenous systems of settlement placement in the Andes. As a result of this forced resettlement of the Andean populations, the current population distribution and settlement pattern of the Province of Paruro cannot be assumed to reflect indigenous systems of spatial, social, or economic organization. Accordingly, the prehistoric regional subsistence-settlement systems of the Province of Paruro are best discerned through archaeological investigations.

Ecological Zones of the Research Region

The steep gradient of the Andean mountains produces a series of diverse climatic zones along its slopes (Gade 1975; Brush 1976). In general, the steeper the gradient of the mountain slope, the more compact the climatic zones. Regions such as the Province of Paruro, where the elevation can drop from 4,300 masl to 2,400 masl across only 6 km, present a broad range of environmental zones in a relatively small area.

Extensive descriptions of the character and composition of Andean climatic zones have been produced by a number of scholars, including Weberbauer (1945), Tosi (1960), Pulgar Vidal (1967), and Troll (1968). As in several other archaeological research project publications that discuss changes in late prehistoric settlement patterns in the Andes (Dillehay 1977:398; Earle et al. 1980; LeBlanc 1981:21–28; Hastorf 1983:49–57; Heffernan 1989:47–48), a modified version of Tosi's (1960) altitude-dependent ecological zone classification will be used in this study to describe the various zones of the Province of Paruro. Four climatic zones are found within the Province of Paruro.

1. Apurimac River bottom: approximately 2,600–3,000 masl (Tosi 1960:88, *Bosque Muy Seco; Subtropical*).

The narrow river bottom of the Apurimac River marks the lowest environmental zone in the research area. It is a zone of extreme heat and aridity with a florescence of cacti. Citrus fruits, achira, cotton, aji, and maize are grown in the rocky soils of its floodplain borders. These crops all require irrigation to assure successful harvests. The construction of canals is, however, difficult in this zone as the tributaries of the Apurimac cut deeply into the mountain slope (Plate 1).

2. Lower tributary valleys: approximately 3,000–3,400 masl (Tosi 1960:101, *Bosque Seco; Montano Bajo*).

The most agriculturally productive and intensively cultivated environmental areas in the Province of Paruro are the bottomlands

Plate 1. The Apurimac River Bottom near the Community of Nayhua

and lower sides of the major tributaries of the Apurimac River. The mild climate and high productivity of this zone, especially in the Paruro Valley, are frequently compared to those of the well-known Urubamba Valley by the local inhabitants. Maize predominates as the primary crop of this zone, although a variety of crops, including various grains, beans, and potatoes, are grown in scattered areas. Where possible, irrigation water is taken from side streams that flow from the more humid puna areas (Plate 2).

3. Upper valley slopes: approximately 3,400–3,900 masl (Tosi 1960:109, *Bosque Húmedo; Montano*).

The concentration of maize cultivation in the tributary bottomland is gradually replaced on the tributary slopes by a variety of Old and New World crops. Gade, working in the Urubamba Valley, writes: "In the Inca period, this zone was undoubtedly characterized by tuber cultivations as well as by native seed crops. Today, *oca, añu, ullucu, quinoa,* and *tarwi* are of a very minor significance in the agricultural and domestic economy" (1975:105–106). Cultivation in this zone is currently dominated by wheat, broad beans, and potatoes (Gade 1975:105). Harvests vary greatly from year to year, however, since these crops are frequently damaged by frost or hail. As frost effectively limits the distribution of maize, its cultivation in this zone is restricted to well-protected *quebradas* or small tertiary river valleys.

Most cultivation on the upper valley slopes is conducted through dryland farming, yet, where possible, small-scale irrigation canals are constructed from springs or streams. The residual soils of the valley slopes contain poorly developed topsoil and require long fallow periods.[3] After one to three years of production, lands must lie fallow from three to twelve years to regenerate. At higher elevations where Andean tuber crops dominate, the fields will frequently be abandoned, not because of decreasing yields, but because of worm infestation. The need for long fallow systems in the Province of Paruro dictates that only a small portion of the upper valley landscape can be cultivated during any one year (Plate 3).

4. Puna: approximately 3,900–4,400 masl (Tosi 1960:122).

This high environmental zone is characterized in the Province of Paruro by rolling hills, rounded ridges, and scattered rock outcrops. The lower reaches of this zone are occasionally used for tuber cultivation (3,900–4,000 masl), while the upper reaches are covered with the hearty Andean ichu grass used extensively for pasture. Gade

Plate 2. The Town of Paruro, Located in a Lower Tributary Valley of the Apurimac

Plate 3. Areas of Potato Cultivation on the Upper Valley Slopes

(1975:104) writes of this zone: "Undoubtedly the most important single grass species is *Stipa ichu*, the basic food of llamas and alpacas, as well as a plant used directly by man in a number of ways. The low temperatures and short growing season rule out full-scale agriculture, and in this zone one finds the uppermost limits of crop cultivation." A variety of frost-resistant tubers are cultivated in the Province of Paruro, including various "sweet" and "bitter" potatoes. From June to August, when the nights are cold and frosts frequent, chuño and *moraya*, two different forms of freeze-dried potatoes, are produced in this zone (Plate 4).

Rising above the upper limits of crop cultivation stand several important mountain peaks, including Seratachin of Pacariqtambo, Masca of Yaurisque, Imanco of Araypallpa, Yauri of Colcha, Pumawasi of San Lorenzo, and Sihuina of Accha. These peaks are known as *apus*, maleficent mountain lords that watch over the communities of the region.

Modern Subsistence-Settlement Systems in the Province of Paruro

The deep V-shaped valleys of the Apurimac River and several of its tributaries, including the Paruro River and the Molle Molle River, provide little area for settlement. The majority of the habitations in the Province of Paruro are located (1) halfway up steep valley sides on isolated spits of flat terrain, (2) in the wider bottomlands of the Apurimac River's secondary tributaries, or (3) on relatively flat areas on the valley sides of the secondary tributaries. The discontinuous settlement pattern of the region is characterized by relatively small and widely scattered villages. In addition, the steep slopes of the Apurimac River Valley and those of its larger tributaries present major barriers to regional communication (Escobar Moscoso 1980:669). The Apurimac River may be forded in selected places, but this is only true from July through September in the dry season. During the annual rains, which last from December to February, the Apurimac River can double in volume and regional communication is limited.

The region of the Apurimac River is thinly populated and agricultural land is of poor quality (Escobar Moscoso 1980). As noted by Poole (1984:82), the only locations in the Province of Paruro where cultivable stretches of land can be found along the Apurimac River are Pillpinto, Colcha, Cusibamba, and Nayhua, none of which has very extensive cultivation. While maize is grown at each of these locations, the production is limited and susceptible to droughts. Poole notes the important effect that the relative lack of valley bottomland in the

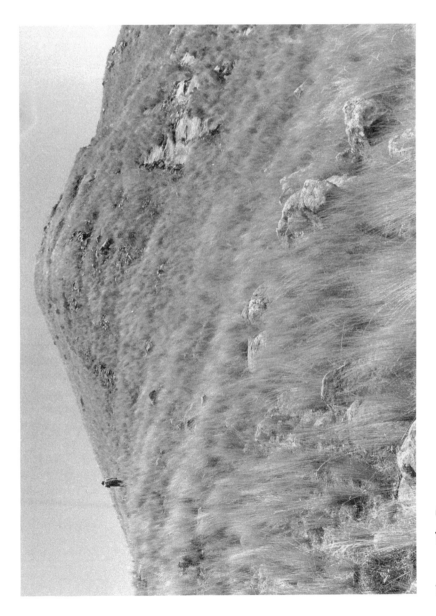

Plate 4. The Puna

Apurimac River Valley—as compared to the expansive flood plain of the Urubamba River Valley—has had on the regional agricultural economy of the Province of Paruro: "In addition to limiting the amount of bottom land available for intensive cultivation, the steep configuration of the Apurimac gorge effectively precludes efficient distribution of irrigation water to the higher terraced fields. As a result, agriculture in the Apurimac and surrounding river valleys has been less focused on the intensive maize cultivation characteristic of the Urubamba region, and more reliant on exploitation of diverse (vertical) productive zones while retaining maize as its primary crop" (Poole 1984:82).

In an effort to exploit a diverse set of resources, members of several communities in the Province of Paruro conduct short migrations, of three to six months, to different ecological zones. For example, each year members of the village of Ccoipa (3,200 masl) move from the maize- and grain-producing zones of their communities into a high mountain valley (3,900 masl) called Hatun Pampa to grow tubers and pasture cattle. On the other side of the survey region, a similar migration is made by certain members of the town of Paruro (3,050 masl), who travel to the protected mountain shelf of Puca Puca (3,950 masl), to concentrate on potato cultivation. Likewise, members of the Mollebamba community undertake short seasonal shifts in residence, moving from the village location (3,300 masl), surrounded by maize fields, to higher areas to cultivate potatoes. During the occupation of the upland zones, residency is maintained through a series of small, widely scattered dwellings. Since, in reality, not all families can gain control of land in all of the ecological zones of the region, small-scale intraregional trade also occurs. This trade is most notable between the villages located in the lowest reaches of the region, with access to citrus fruit, and the higher villages, which generally contain large areas of potato production.

The region's own resources are also supplemented by traditional, small-scale trade relations between various communities of the Province of Paruro and the Province of Chumbivilcas. The Province of Chumbivilcas, a uniformly higher region located to the south of the Province of Paruro but still in the Department of Cuzco, contains a large number of dispersed, pastoral communities. Each year, usually after the maize harvests are completed in the Province of Paruro, groups from Chumbivilcas, often accompanied by herds of llamas, will walk three to eight days to specific communities in Paruro where they have established traditional trading partners to exchange meat and wool for agricultural products.

The Province of Paruro, in summary, contains a number of steep valleys and closely compressed ecological zones that extend from the hot and arid Apurimac River bottom at 2,500 masl to the cold, wind-swept mountaintop of Pumawasi at 4,428 masl. The steep V-shaped valley of the Apurimac River, while providing a wide variety of ecological zones in a relatively short distance, has limited the range of agricultural techniques applicable to the region and has restricted regional communication and transportation. The population of the Province of Paruro has responded to this situation through the development of relatively isolated and self-sufficient communities. In addition, each of the major reducción villages simultaneously exploits diverse sets of resources, ranging from the citrus fruits of the river bottom to high-altitude grasses. Some transhumance does occur as families, or groups of men, change residence from villages in temperate zones to scattered settlements in the upper reaches of potato cultivation for four to six months of the year.[4] In Chapter 6 it will be shown that similar systems of resource exploitation were already developed and in use in the Province of Paruro during both the Killke and Inca periods.

The Pre-Hispanic Road Network South of Cuzco

Archaeological surveys and historical research provide information on the Inca road network that linked the city of Cuzco with the ethnic groups living in the Province of Paruro (Map 5). During our regional survey work in the Province of Paruro all of these roads were walked and the remains of cobblestones, terraces, and steps were noted. The roads continue to be in use today, although they are no longer systematically maintained.

The major road leading south of Cuzco directly into the survey region is referred to in the chronicles as *El Camino Real de Cuntisuyu* (the Royal Road of Cuntisuyu). The road left Cuzco through Belén, a southern sector of the city, which has long been associated with Cuntisuyu (Sarmiento de Gamboa [1572, Bk. 11] 1906:34). The road, which is still a major footpath of the region, traveled due south of Cuzco along the Huancaro River and then crossed the Ocopata/Llaulliccasa Pass (+4,000 masl). After passing this rich region of potato production, it dropped to the site of the modern town of Yaurisque. The Royal Road of Cuntisuyu then continued south, traversing the length of the Paruro River. Just north of the modern community of Paruro it crossed the present archaeological site of Tantar Cuzco, continuing south to the Cusibamba flood plain along the bank of the Apurimac River.

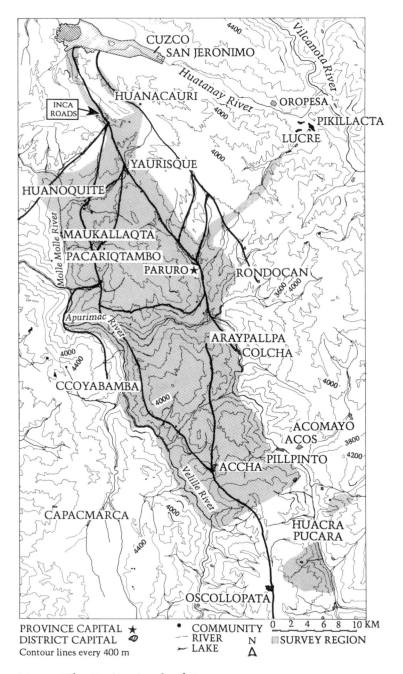

PROVINCE CAPITAL ★	• COMMUNITY	0 2 4 6 8 10 KM
DISTRICT CAPITAL 🏘	-- RIVER	N
Contour lines every 400 m	⌣ LAKE	▲	▦ SURVEY REGION

Map 5. The Region South of Cuzco

The course of the Royal Road of Cuntisuyu is clearly described by Cristóbal de Molina (de Cuzco) in his account of the August purification rite of *citua*.[5] Molina (1575) writes that during this ritual cleaning of Cuzco, runners left the city carrying ashes along the royal roads of the four regional suyus.. The ashes were passed along the royal suyu roads by a series of runners until they reached the major rivers of the Cuzco region.

Los que iban a la parte de Contisuyo eran de las generaciones siguientes: Yauri panaca ayllo, China panaca ayllo, Masca panaca ayllo y Quesco ayllo; y éstos los allegaban a Churicalla, que es dos leguas del Cuzco, y allí las entregaban a los *mitimaes* de Yaurisqui, que será tres leguas del Cuzco, y éstos las entregaban a los de Tantar, que es cuatro leguas del Cuzco, y aquéllos las llegaban al río de Cusibamba, que es donde los frailes de la Merced tienen una viña, que es siete leguas del Cuzco; y allí se bañaban y lavaban las armas. (Molina [1575] 1943:32)

Those who went toward Cuntisuyu were from the following lineages: Yaura Panaca[6] Ayllu, China Panaca Ayllu, Masca Panaca Ayllu, and Quesco Ayllu. They ran as far as Churicalla, which is two leagues from Cuzco, and there they delivered the ashes to the *mitimaes* (colonists) of Yaurisque, which must be about three leagues from Cuzco. The mitimaes passed them on to those of Tantar Cuzco, which is four leagues from Cuzco, who carried them on to the river of Cusibamba, where the Friars of the Merced have a vineyard. This is seven leagues from Cuzco, and there they bathed and washed their weapons.[7]

While the citua purification ritual ended at the Apurimac River, the Royal Road of Cuntisuyu did not. From the Cusibamba plain it crossed the Apurimac River on a suspension bridge called Huarancalla (Plate 5).[8] Immediately after the suspension bridge the road divided: a lower branch led to the Colcha region while the major, upper branch climbed its way to the area of Araypallpa. Leaving Araypallpa, the royal road continued south into the Pampacucho Valley. From Pampacucho it crossed over the pass and then dropped to the plain of Accha.

A number of other important Inca roads also crossed the Province of Paruro. For example, travelers walking from Cuzco to the site of Maukallaqta could have followed the Royal Road of Cuntisuyu to Yaurisque and then turned west and followed the Yaurisque River to the small Inca site of Huaynacancha. A more direct route from Cuzco to Maukallaqta led across a high open plain to the south of Llaulli-

Plate 5. Modern Highway Bridge and Old Suspension Bridge of Huarancalla over the Apurimac River

ccasa and descended directly into the Yaurisque River Valley near Huaynacancha. Both of these routes would have led the visitor first to Huaynacancha. The place is mentioned by several Spanish sources in connection with the Inca origin myth (Pardo 1946; Urton 1989, 1990; Bauer 1991). Murúa calls it Guaynac Cancha ([1615, Bk. 1, Chap. 2] 1962:21). Cabello Balboa calls it Guamancancha ([1586, Part III, Chap. 9] 1951:261), and Sarmiento de Gamboa writes Guanacancha ([1572, Chap. 12] 1906:35). From Huaynacancha a trail zigzagged up the steep slope of the Huaynacancha Quebrada to Maukallaqta.

Another trail led from Yaurisque into the Pacariqtambo area. This trail, called the *Chaupi Ñan* (Middle Way), formed the division between the Hanan and Hurin moieties of the Tambo ethnic group (Urton 1984, 1989, 1990).[9] The road crossed the Apurimac River near Nayhua, which apparently was a ford, and continued southward into the region of Chumbivilcas.

Crossing the northern border of the Province of Paruro is another important trail, referred to as the *Camino Blanco* (White Road). This road leaves Cuzco to the southeast and travels up the Tancarpata Valley. Passing just south of Huanacauri, the road passes through a high region (4,000 masl) to the village of Mayumbamba. At Mayumbamba the trail continues into the region of the Quehuare and Papres ethnic groups, while two smaller branches drop into the Paruro River Valley.

The Camino Real de Cuntisuyu, the Chaupi Ñan, and the Camino Blanco connected the Inca Period settlements of the Province of Paruro with Cuzco. In addition, there were scores of secondary trails that connected the many small communities of the region to each other. As will be seen in Chapter 6, there is little change between the Killke and Inca period settlement patterns in the Province of Paruro. The fact that the Inca Period and the Killke Period settlement patterns for the region are very similar and that the major sites are located along the same road network suggests that the road system of the region was well established before the development of the Inca state.

Research Methodology

A research methodology based primarily on systematic survey data was selected for this project with the belief that the developmental processes of state formation are best investigated through regional archaeological investigations (Hutterer and Macdonald 1982:163). Regional archaeological surveys suppose that the spatial distribution of sites of a prehistoric society will reflect the fundamental organizational features of that society, and that a systematic examination of site types, locations, and sizes in a region is a logical beginning point in the investigation of prehistoric social and economic systems. As Hutterer and Macdonald write (1982:162), "... the settlement approach in archaeology discards the notion of 'typical' or 'key' sites and concentrates instead on the *range* of archaeological sites and other phenomena found within a region, and the spatial *patterns* they form for a given prehistoric period." Assuming that the site settlement patterns in a region reflect indigenous patterns of resource use, subsistence procurement, and social organization, archaeological surveys are now recognized as the necessary first stage in most regional research programs in the Andes (Browman 1970; Earle et al. 1980; Parsons and Hastings 1977; Wilson 1988) and elsewhere (Parsons 1972; Ammerman 1981).

Regional Survey Boundaries and Survey Procedures

The study area, a total of 600 km[2], extends from the ruins of Huanacauri near Cuzco in the north to the town of Accha, 42 aerial kilometers to the south. It is bounded on the west by the Velille and Molle Molle rivers; on the east it includes the drainage system of the Paruro River, and farther south it is bounded by the Apurimac River (Maps 5 and 6). Systematic survey work conducted in this portion of the Province of Paruro covered the majority of the territory thought to have been controlled by the Masca, Chillque, and Tambo.

The archaeological research was accomplished following guidelines provided by Parsons and Hastings (1977) for regional survey work in the Andes. The goal of this fieldwork was to identify the locations of all prehistoric habitation sites and support facilities in the research zone. This information was used to establish subsistence-settlement patterns for the Killke and Inca populations of the region. To conduct the survey, teams of two to three persons, spaced at 50- to 150-m intervals, walked assigned areas and identified the locations of prehistoric settlements and related features, such as roads, terraces, and bridges.[10] The sites in the research region generally consisted of pottery scatters and lacked standing architecture.[11] When a site was found, its location was marked on enlarged aerial photographs (approximate scale 1:10,000) and on topographic maps (scale 1:25,000) that the surveyors carried while in the field. Standardized survey forms were completed and photographs were taken of each site. When sites containing structural remains were found they were mapped with the aid of Brunton pocket transits and 25-m measuring tapes.[12]

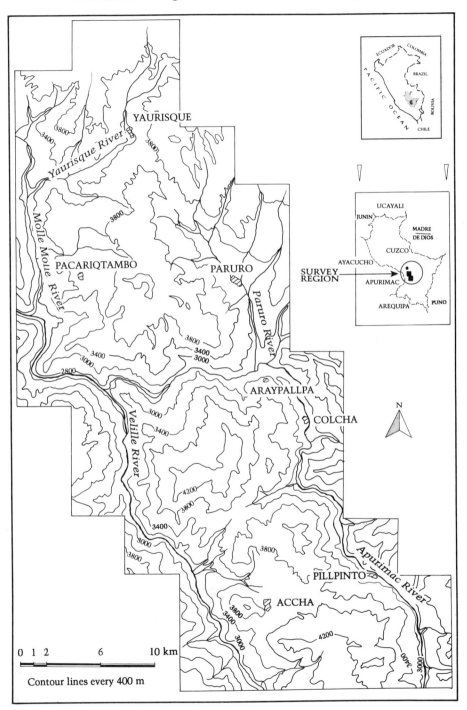

Map 6. The Survey Region

Regional Coverage

The survey was designed for complete coverage of the study region. As in the work of Parsons and Hastings (1977:11) in the Upper Mantaro region, this survey of the Province of Paruro systemically covered the valley floors and lower valley slopes, the ridges and mountaintops and their upper adjacent slopes, and the low- to medium-gradient slopes of the region. The extremely steep slopes, which were dangerous to cross, were not systematically examined, except where access could be gained through local trails. It may be concluded that the exclusion of these areas from the fieldwork probably does not present a significant bias in the data collection, since the steepness of the slopes, which discouraged survey work, also would have limited prehistoric activities or occupations.

It should be noted, however, that the implementation of systematic regional surveys in an Andean setting is complicated by variations in surface visibility in different ecological zones. Territory in grain-producing zones generally provides good to excellent conditions for surface surveys. The land is relatively free of ground-covering plants such as grass, and many areas are cultivated with scratch plows, which bring artifacts to the surface. Other ecological zones present very different surface conditions, complicating the process of locating and dating sites. For example, ridges and mountaintops are rarely cultivated, and surface artifacts in these locations are constantly exposed to weathering processes (Parsons and Hastings 1977:12). The eroded nature of surface pottery at these sites often makes cultural identification difficult. Also, the high puna areas of the research region are frequently covered with thick wild grasses, leaving few ground areas visible.[13]

Another difficulty in achieving true 100 percent coverage of the survey region was the presence of several relatively large towns, such as Paruro, Yaurisque, and Accha, and numerous small villages, such as Nayhua, Araypallpa, Ayusbamba, Colcha, and Ccoipa. As a result of modern construction and land use, only limited areas in these communities could be surveyed. To support the limited coverage of these locations, interviews were held with principal informants concerning archaeological finds in each community. In some of the towns, such as Accha, and in several of the small villages, archaeological sites were detected and surface collections were made, although the exact dimensions of these sites were difficult to estimate. Because the areas covered by the modern towns of the region represent a very small proportion of the total research region, and because limited surface surveys were conducted in the majority of them, their presence does not seriously affect the overall data base for the region.[14]

Pottery Collections

Pottery samples were collected at each site and then analyzed to determine the periods of site occupation. During the ceramic collection process, the team of surveyors systematically walked over the surface of the site in parallel lines, approximately 5 m apart, collecting pottery fragments. If architectural units or field boundaries were present at the site, separate collections were made in each unit. After the collections were completed, the pottery was examined. The diagnostic fragments were retained, while the undiagnostic fragments were removed from the collection and left at the site. This preliminary pottery sort was necessitated by the remoteness of the research area and the difficulties in transporting the pottery collections by horse to the nearest road. Exceptions were made at sites that yielded a relatively small number of surface fragments. In these cases all the pottery shards were retained and reexamined in Cuzco.[15]

Initial reconnaissance work in the study area during 1982 and 1983 indicated that the previously established Cuzco pottery sequence for the later periods of prehistory could be used to date the prehistoric occupations of the Province of Paruro. The literature on Inca ceramics (Bingham 1915a; Eaton 1916; Valcárcel Vizquerra 1934, 1935; Pardo 1938, 1939, 1957; Rowe 1944; Baca Cosio 1974, 1989; Alcina Franch et al. 1976; Kendall 1976; Lunt 1987) and Inca architecture (Rowe 1944; Kendall 1974, 1985; Gasparini and Margolies 1980; Niles 1980, 1987) provided a means to identify the Inca remains of the region. Rowe's (1944) and Dwyer's (1971) introductory work on Killke pottery and subsequent research reports by Rivera Dorado (1971a, 1971b, 1972, 1973), Kendall (1974, 1976, 1985), and Lunt (1987) aided in dating the Killke Period occupations of the region. In addition, classification of the artifact collections was also aided by conversations with Gordon McEwan, Sara Lunt, and Arminda Gibaja Oviedo, as well as with members of the Universidad Nacional San Antonio Abad del Cuzco, including Luis Barreda Murillo, Alfredo Valencia Zegarra, and Manuel Chávez Ballón.[16]

Excavations

To provide complementary information to the regional survey data, a limited excavation program was carried out in the Province of Paruro. In 1986, a number of rooms were excavated at the site of Maukallaqta (Chapter 7). The primary goals of this work were to collect information concerning the room functions and to test for pre-Inca remains beneath the site. The Maukallaqta excavations were conducted using arbitrary 10-cm levels until stratigraphy was found and were continued until sterile subsoil was reached. A 1-by-1-m grid system was laid out in relatively large structures, while a 50-by-50-cm grid system was used in the smaller rooms.

During the course of the investigations in the Province of Paruro, test squares were also conducted at a number of smaller sites. These excavations, consisting of 2-by-2-m or 2-by-4-m pits in fields or along ridgetops, were made to test for subsurface remains and to further develop the Cuzco ceramic sequence. It was especially important to understand the temporal relationship between Killke pottery and a newly identified ceramic style called "Colcha" (Chapter 5). These test excavations, like those at Maukallaqta, were conducted using 10-cm levels and were terminated when sterile subsoil was reached. All artifacts recovered in the course of this fieldwork were transported to Cuzco for laboratory analysis.[17]

Previous Ethnographic and Historical Studies in the Province of Paruro

Archaeological research in the Province of Paruro has been facilitated by a number of ethnographic and historical studies that have been recently completed. Fortunately, this region became the focus of a series of independent ethnographic and historical research projects just before and during the period of this fieldwork. As a result of these studies, the Province of Paruro, which up to the early 1980s was one of the least known provinces in the Department of Cuzco, has now become one of the most intensely studied regions. To date, major ethnographic and/or historical projects have been conducted in five of the nine district capitals, including Accha (Decoster 1989), Colcha (Poole 1984), Huanoquite (Seligmann 1987), Pacariqtambo (Urton 1984, 1985, 1986, 1988, 1989, 1990), and Paruro (Poole 1984). These studies have provided ethnographic and historical information for the Province of Paruro at a level that is currently unavailable for any other area in the Department of Cuzco.

Following the presentation of the theoretical concerns of this work in the first chapter and essential chronological and background information in Chapters 2 through 4, the archaeological data collected from the Province of Paruro will next be presented and analyzed. In the following chapter the distribution patterns of two ceramic types will be examined for indications of regional interactions and exchange during the period of state development. The definition of these ceramic types and analyses of their distribution across the Province of Paruro provide necessary information for the discussions presented in Chapters 6, 7, and 8. In these later chapters, the economic and social organizations of the region's ethnic groups on the eve of, and during, the expansion of the Inca state will be examined.

5.

Killke Period Pottery Production and Exchange in the Cuzco Region

KILLKE POTTERY, as the immediate antecedent to Inca pottery, holds a unique and important position in the history of the Cuzco region. Changes in the production and distribution of this ceramic style through time provide archaeologists with a means to examine the development of the Inca state in the Cuzco region.[1] Surface collections and test excavations conducted in the Province of Paruro have documented the presence of Killke pottery south of the Cuzco Valley as well as a new Killke-related ceramic style named "Colcha." The purpose of this chapter is to describe the Killke and Colcha pottery styles and to discuss their separate distribution patterns in the survey region. By examining the nature of Killke Period regional interaction and exchange relationships, as reflected by ceramic distribution patterns, insights are gained into the social and economic conditions of the region during the period of state formation. This chapter begins with a summary of the current state of Killke ceramic studies in the Cuzco region. In the second section, Killke pottery and the new Killke-related style, Colcha pottery, are described.[2] Survey data are then analyzed along with excavation results and historical and ethnographic information in an effort to determine the temporal and spatial relationships that existed between these two related ceramic styles. In the fourth section, the distribution patterns of the Killke and Colcha ceramic materials in the Province of Paruro are discussed as they relate to the regional social and economic conditions in which early state development took place.

Review of Killke Research

Among the earliest known excavations conducted in the Department of Cuzco were those of Max Uhle (1912) at the site of Q'atan, in the Urubamba River Valley. These excavations and additional collections made by Uhle in the Cuzco region produced a style of pottery quite different from styles generally associated with the Inca. Since little was known of the pre–Inca Period of the Department of Cuzco, Uhle could only suggest that this new pottery style dated to a pre-Inca, but post-Tiahuanaco, period, and he proposed a broad A.D. 800 to A.D. 1400 time frame. Soon after Uhle's discovery, Jacinto Jijón y Caamaño and Carlos Larrea M. (1918) reproduced Uhle's findings in their article "Un cementerio incaico en Quito." Later, in *Los orígenes del Cuzco*, Jijón y Caamaño (1934) again reproduced some of Uhle's material and presented additional examples of similar ceramics that he found in the Cuzco region and in museum collections. Like Uhle, Jijón y Caamaño suggested a broad pre-Inca, post-Tiahuanaco time period for the production of this new ceramic style. These isolated finds by Uhle and Jijón y Caamaño would later be classified as Killke-related ceramics and dated to the immediate pre–Inca Period of the Cuzco region (Rowe 1944:61–62).

In 1941 Rowe began a survey of the Cuzco Valley and undertook a series of test excavations. Although earlier research in the region had focused on explorations and site descriptions, Rowe's work represented the first systematic archaeological research project within the Department of Cuzco. One goal of this research was to identify and describe the pre-Inca ceramic sequence for the Cuzco region (Rowe 1944:61). Test excavations conducted by Rowe in a courtyard of the monastery of Santo Domingo, near the Inca "Temple of the Sun" (Coricancha), revealed an undisturbed deposit containing ceramic materials similar to those previously found by Uhle and Jijón y Caamaño (Rowe 1944:61–62). Additional surface collections made by Rowe later that year at a number of archaeological sites in the Cuzco region showed that this new pottery style was present in the city of Cuzco, and was widely distributed throughout the valley.

Rowe performed test excavations in and around the city of Cuzco during 1942 and 1943 to investigate further the new ceramic style, which by then had been named "Killke."[3] The recovery of large quantities of Killke pottery at the site of Sacsahuaman, just north of the city of Cuzco, was especially important in this research. Through the use of the Sacsahuaman materials, Rowe developed a broad stylistic typology for what he called the "Killke Series" (Rowe 1944:60–62). Although he did not find stratified Killke and Inca deposits, he inferred, on the basis of his surface collections, that Killke pottery was the antecedent to Inca pottery in the Cuzco Valley (Rowe 1944:61).

The identification of an Early Inca ceramic type in the Cuzco Valley had a profound impact on the study of the Inca. Imperial Inca pottery of the Cuzco region had long been recognized (Bingham 1915b; Eaton 1916; Valcárcel Vizquerra 1934, 1935; Pardo 1938, 1939). The discovery of a precursor to this pottery style provided a means to identify sites occupied during the early development of the Inca state. Future excavations of sites dating to the Early Inca Period would yield information on the social and economic conditions in which state development took place.

Rowe (1944, 1945) suggests that the transition from Killke (or Early Inca) pottery to Inca pottery occurred during a period of rapid state development. This transition period has been equated with the rule of Pachacuti Inca Yupanqui, which is thought to have begun in A.D. 1438 (see Chapters 1 and 3). Using the dynastic list of Inca kings provided by Cabello Balboa (1586), Rowe (1944:57) has also written that the mythical founding of Cuzco took place around A.D. 1250, a date that he and others correlate with the beginning of the Killke pottery tradition.[4]

Soon after Rowe's formal identification of the Killke style, Jorge Muelle led an expedition into the Province of Paruro. Near the Hacienda of Ayusbamba, in the District of Pacariqtambo, Muelle identified three sites that contained pottery similar to the Killke materials identified by Rowe in the Cuzco Valley (Muelle 1945). Muelle's recovery of Killke materials outside the immediate confines of the Cuzco Valley suggested that Killke-style pottery was distributed throughout the entire region. Despite this discovery and the immediate academic acceptance of Killke pottery as the Early Inca pottery style in the Cuzco region, an extensive study of Killke pottery was not conducted for another twenty years.

From 1966 to 1968, Edward Dwyer conducted excavations at three sites in the Cuzco region: Minas Pata in the Lucre Basin, Pucara Pantillijlla near Pisac, and Sacsahuaman. The purpose of Dwyer's research was to further investigate the Killke Series as earlier defined by Rowe. Of the three sites selected for excavation, Sacsahuaman again provided the largest sample of Killke-style pottery, and carbon extracted from a hearth in a Killke context yielded a radiocarbon age of A.D. 1180 ± 140.[5] Using this radiocarbon date, Dwyer (1971:140) set the beginning of Killke pottery production slightly earlier than Rowe, writing, "Killke culture was probably dominant in the Valley of Cuzco from around 1100 A.D. until the establishment of the Inca Empire."

Since Rowe's initial work and Dwyer's detailed study of Killke ceramics, a number of other archaeological projects have noted the presence of Killke and Killke-related ceramics in the Cuzco region. Miguel Rivera Dorado (1971a, 1971b, 1972, 1973), for example, describes Killke and Killke-related materials recovered in excavations at the sites of Cancha-Cancha and Chacomoqo in the Chinchero area. This region is thought by many to have been occupied by a large and powerful group of Inca de Privilegio called the Ayarmaca (Rostworowski de Diez Canseco 1970). Kenneth Heffernan (1989), working in the Limatambo area to the west of Cuzco, has found Killke and Killke-related materials at a large number of sites. Ann Kendall (1974, 1976, 1985) presents examples of Killke and Killke-related pottery recovered during excavations and surface collections in the Cusichaca Valley, in the lower drainage system of the Vilcanota/Urubamba River, and Sara Lunt (1983, 1987) provides a detailed study of Inca, Killke, and Killke-related ceramic wares from the same region. In addition, Luis Barreda Murillo (1973), Arminda Gibaja Oviedo (1983), and Gordon McEwan (1983, 1984, 1987) report the presence of Killke pottery in the Lucre Basin southeast of Cuzco, within the territory of a large group of Inca de Privilegio called the Muyna, as well as the presence of a poorly defined, Killke-related style named "Lucre." Gibaja Oviedo (pers. com. 1987) also reports finding Killke pottery at Pisac and Ollantaytambo, in the Vilcanota/Urubamba River Valley, while José Gonzales Corrales (1985) describes finding Killke materials in his excavations within the city of Cuzco. Furthermore, Alfredo Valencia Zegarra, Manuel Chávez Ballón, and Italo Oberti Rodríguez have each identified Killke remains in the Cuzco region (pers. coms. 1987). From these various studies it can be concluded that Killke and Killke-related pottery styles are widely distributed across the Cuzco region; however, the nature of the distribution remains to be investigated.

Description of Killke Pottery

Most archaeologists working in the Cuzco region and using the preliminary descriptions of Killke pottery provided by Rowe (1944) and Dwyer (1971) agree on the broad elements of the Killke ceramic style, even though they may disagree over the classification of individual examples. In this book, building on the ceramic descriptions provided by Rowe (1944) and Dwyer (1971), as well as those of Kendall (1976) and Lunt (1987), the following criteria have been used to identify Killke pottery.

Ware

Killke pottery is composed of a medium-coarse fabric containing a moderate quantity of nonplastic inclusions varying in size from 0.01 to 0.25 mm. These inclusions vary in color from an ashy white to a dull, dark gray. The inclusions appear to be high in feldspar, although the presence of quartz and chert, as well as andesite, amphibole, arkose, and syenite has also been noted (Lunt pers. com. 1987). The clean clay matrix suggests that the clay was washed, and a bimodal grain size distribution of the nonplastic inclusions suggests that temper was added (Lunt pers. com. 1989). The ware is medium-hard and the surface of the vessel frequently fires to a buff or salmon-pink color.

Vessel Forms

The known vessel forms for Killke pottery have been discussed by Dwyer (1971). Killke vessel forms include both straight- and curved-sided bowls, as well as incurving bowls and straight-sided plates. Three different types of medium-sized, single-handled jars have also been identified, including jars with high-arching handles, jars with faces portrayed on their necks (Face Neck Jars), and jars with conical necks (Dwyer 1971; Bauer 1990a; Bauer and Stanish 1990). Large Killke jars frequently have ovoid bodies, concave necks, and paired handles. In addition, straight-sided cups, or *keros* (also called "tumblers," Dwyer 1971:100), are also found within Killke collections.

Design Elements and Pigment Color

Decorations on Killke vessels are generally geometric in form and composition (Fig. 6). Narrow lines, thicker bands, triangles, and diamonds are the most common design elements. Black is the most frequently used color, followed by red and, rarely, white. Dwyer writes: "The white and black colors are uniformly consistent, and the red varies from deep purple to pink depending upon conditions of application and firing. There are never two shades of red on one vessel. These colors are all painted on unpigmented buff slip background. The only exception to this rule is the occasional use of white as a background" (Dwyer 1971:104).

Among the wide variety of design motifs used in Killke pottery, the most frequent are broad red or occasionally black bands outlined by one to three narrow black lines. Other motifs include sets of nested triangles that often alternate in color from red to black, linked ovals with central dots, linked rectangles with solid interior ovals, large areas covered with black cross-hatching, cross-hatched diamonds, and pendant rows of solid or cross-hatched triangles. (See Fig. 6, col. 1, as well as Dwyer 1971 and Rowe 1944, Fig. 19:11–21, for examples of Killke pottery found in the Cuzco Valley. See Fig. 6, cols. 2 and 3, and Bauer 1990a, Figs. 35–47, for examples of Killke pottery recovered in the Province of Paruro.)

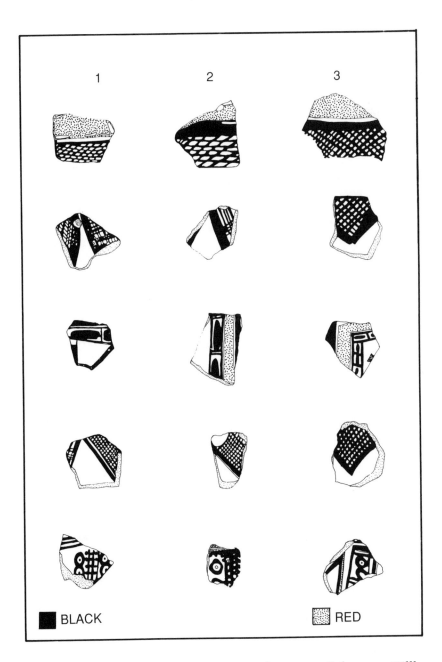

Figure 6. Killke Pottery from Cuzco and Paruro: *Column 1*, Killke Pottery from the Cuzco Valley (after Rowe 1944: 16, fig. 1; 19, figs. 11, 12, 16, and 21); *Columns 2 and 3*, Killke Pottery from the Province of Paruro

Surface Treatment and Pigment Application Techniques

The exterior and interior surfaces of Killke bowls and the exterior of other Killke vessels are covered with a slip of smoothed body clay. The surfaces are then burnished, producing a medium-gloss effect (Dwyer 1971:87).

Designs on Killke pottery frequently display low-to-medium color-tone contrast. This appears to result from the use of watery pigments. In addition, the edges of Killke designs often appear blurred, a characteristic that may be caused by a slight absorption of the thin pigments by the surface of the vessel (Lunt pers. com. 1988). There is also a certain "characteristic carelessness of execution" compared to the fine Inca ceramics that most likely developed out of the Killke tradition (Rowe 1944:49). This is most clearly apparent in the broad and apparently quickly executed brushstrokes of the vessel designs, which often leave undulating bands, as well as in the frequent overlapping of adjacent designs.

Description of Colcha Pottery

While we were conducting our archaeological surveys in the Province of Paruro, it soon became apparent that, besides Killke pottery, a second, closely related pottery style was also present in the region. Since the density of sites with this new pottery appeared to increase as we surveyed the District of Colcha, the style was named "Colcha." Examples of Colcha pottery collected in the course of our surveys are provided in Figure 7 as well as in Bauer (1990a, Figs. 48–60). The new pottery style of Colcha is defined as a Killke-related style, since it shares many stylistic similarities with Killke pottery. Colcha pottery can, however, be distinguished from Killke pottery through (1) a much coarser paste composition; (2) the extensive use of a chalky, white slip; and, to a lesser extent, (3) the use of design motifs that have not been identified as belonging to Killke pottery. The differences and similarities between Killke and Colcha pottery are outlined below.

Ware

Killke pottery has been described as containing a medium-coarse fabric with nonplastic inclusions that vary in size from 0.01 to 0.25 mm. Colcha pottery contains a sharply contrasting paste with a coarse fabric and a large quantity of nonplastic inclusions. Granitic inclusions are the most frequent and can vary greatly in size from 0.01 to 2.0 mm. The paste of Colcha pottery is of moderate hardness and con-

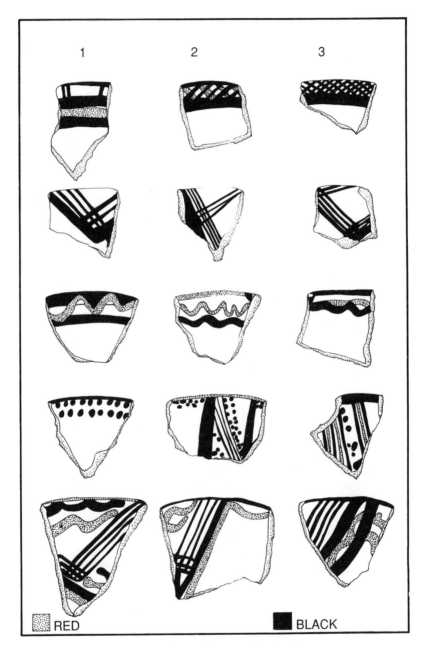

Figure 7. Colcha Pottery from the Province of Paruro

tains scattered single grains of black and gold mica, as well as free quartz, feldspar, and biotite. Many casts are altered, and tiny clay pellets are present (Lunt pers. com. 1989). The vessel surface frequently fires to a red or orange color.

Vessel Forms

No complete Colcha vessels were found during our survey work south of Cuzco. Vessel fragments suggest, however, that most of the Colcha vessel forms closely resembled those of Killke pottery (Bauer 1990a, App. II).

Design Elements, Color, and Surface Treatment

Geometric design elements predominate in Colcha pottery. The most common of these elements include wavy and straight lines, thicker bands, triangles, diamonds, and cross-hatching. These design elements appear to be nearly identical to those found on Killke pottery, but Colcha pottery also contains a frequent use of dots, a design that is rarely seen in the repertoire of Killke design elements (Bauer 1990a, App. II).

While Killke and Colcha pottery share a common inventory of basic geometric design elements, there are differences in the manner in which these design elements and their composite design motifs are applied to the surface of the ceramic vessel. Both Rowe (1944:60) and Dwyer (1971:104) write that Killke pottery designs are generally applied to unpigmented, frequently burnished ceramic surfaces. The exception to this rule is the occasional use of a white slip. In contrast to the generally unpigmented surface of Killke pottery, a dominant element of Colcha pottery is the presence of a white background slip. Because of this, the surface of Colcha pottery, unlike that of Killke pottery, is rarely burnished. The use of this white slip and thicker pigments in Colcha pottery produces stronger tonal contrasts than are found in Killke pottery. In addition, the slip (which lends a chalky surface to Colcha pottery) seals the porous surface of the ceramic vessels and prevents the absorption of the decorative designs and the edge blurring that are frequently observed in Killke pottery.

The two ceramic styles also vary in their selective use of colors. In Killke pottery, narrow black lines arranged in geometric designs and applied directly to a buff or pink pottery surface are common. In Colcha pottery, black is only occasionally used. Far more common in Colcha pottery, however, is the use of medium- to dark-brown lines painted on white slip. Our sample also indicates that the broad red bands outlined by narrow black lines that are classic hallmarks of the Killke tradition are not present in Colcha pottery. Red, when it is used on Colcha pottery, simply appears in narrow, straight, or wavy lines.

The Relationship between Killke and Colcha Pottery

The temporal and spatial relations between Killke and Colcha pottery need to be examined to determine whether the two pottery styles represent an evolutionary sequence or two ceramic styles produced during the same period. Either one of these possible relationships between Killke and Colcha pottery can have important implications for archaeological research in the Cuzco area. If Colcha pottery is found to predate Killke pottery, new evidence could be presented for a developmental Killke ceramic sequence. The discovery of an antecedent to Killke pottery south of Cuzco might, in turn, support literal readings of the chronicles, which state that ancestors of the Inca migrated to the Cuzco Valley from the Province of Paruro (Brundage 1963:15–18). It is also possible that Colcha pottery developed after Killke pottery and represents a relatively late-prehistoric ceramic tradition in the Cuzco region, which perhaps was concurrent with Inca pottery production.

An alternative explanation is that Killke and Colcha pottery do not represent an evolutionary sequence, but instead are two contemporary ceramic styles. Killke pottery has long been associated with the Cuzco Valley and has been assumed to have been produced there. It is possible that Colcha pottery represents a southern pottery style that was produced in the Province of Paruro contemporaneously with Killke pottery. The identification of a second pottery production center in the Cuzco region during Killke times, but outside of the Cuzco Valley, would lend insight into the production and distribution of regional pottery styles during the Killke Period and could be used to address questions concerning the Inca's relationships with other regional ethnic groups during the period of state formation.

Test Excavation Results

During 1987, test excavations were conducted at different sites in the Province of Paruro to further develop the ceramic sequence for the Cuzco region. An issue of particular importance for this study was the chronological relationship between Killke pottery and the newly discovered Colcha pottery. Limited test excavations were conducted at multicomponent sites in the areas of Yaurisque, Paruro, Pacariqtambo, and Colcha. Unfortunately, like other researchers working in the Cuzco region, we found that the majority of these sites were badly disturbed (Kendall 1974). Inca construction activities, the plowing of the sites by the local population over the course of centuries, and extensive erosion had reduced the contents of the upper soil levels to undifferentiated mixtures containing Inca, Killke, and Colcha pottery. The disturbed nature of these and other sites in the Cuzco region continues to make interpretations of the late-prehistoric pottery sequences difficult.

The most conclusive evidence concerning the relationship between Killke and Colcha pottery was found during test excavations at the site of Tejahuasi. This site is the property of the Paruro-based ayllu Cucuchiráy and is located at an altitude of 3,200 masl on a long, narrow ridge, immediately to the east of the town of Paruro.[6] Although there are no structural remains visible on the surface of the ridge, its slopes are covered with dense concentrations of pottery. Surface collections at the site yielded examples of Inca, Killke, Colcha, and Huari pottery, as well as examples of two new pre-Inca ceramic styles currently under study.[7]

A series of test excavations, each measuring 2 by 4 m, was carried out along the western side of the site. The excavations proceeded through a 20-cm-deep plow zone and then through a deposit of compacted earth, approximately 30 cm deep. The remains of a low-standing stone and clay wall were found in one of the test units at a depth of 56 cm. On the northern side of the wall foundation, a floor level of packed earth, small cobbles, and flat stones was identified (Fig. 8). A deposit of compact dark-brown soil, 30 cm deep, was encountered beneath the floor and above the natural subsoil of the ridge. The deposit contained both Killke and Colcha pottery. A carbon sample from this compact layer of dark-brown soil provided a radiocarbon age of 940 B.P. or A.D. 1010 ± 140, a date similar to that obtained by Dwyer during his excavations of Killke materials at the site of Sacsahuaman near Cuzco.[8]

The stratigraphic sequence at the site of Tejahuasi provides important information for establishing provisional dates for Killke and Colcha pottery production. The stone and clay wall and the adjacent floor represent the last occupational phase of the site, which dates to the Inca Period.[9] Most important for the analysis is, however, the absence of Inca materials below the structure and the sealing of an apparently pre–Inca Period soil deposit, containing both Killke and Colcha pottery, by the construction of a packed earth and stone floor. It should be noted, however, that these observations come from test excavations that, due to their limited coverage, do not always provide definitive results. In addition, the single radiocarbon sample from the site of Tejahuasi has

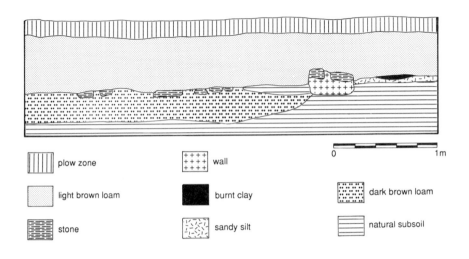

Figure 8. Excavations at Tejahuasi, Profile 1

yielded a large standard deviation. Nevertheless, the presence of both Killke and Colcha pottery in a context beneath a floor indicates that these two related pottery styles may have been both used and produced during the Killke Period.

Surface Survey Evidence

The preliminary excavation data from Tejahuasi indicate that Colcha and Killke pottery may represent two contemporary ceramic styles. Given this provisional finding, it now may be asked whether these two ceramic styles are the products of a single center of pottery production or of two separate centers.[10] If the two ceramic styles were produced in two widely separate centers (e.g., one in the Cuzco Valley and another in the Province of Paruro), then it is probable that their distribution patterns south of Cuzco would not be identical. If, on the other hand, Killke and Colcha pottery were produced by a single production center, the distribution patterns of the two ceramic styles might appear similar in the archaeological record.

To compare the distribution patterns of these two ceramic styles in the Province of Paruro, the distance of each site containing Colcha and/or Killke pottery from Cuzco was calculated (Figs. 9 and 10).[11] The Killke- and Colcha-site number/distance observations were then mathematically compared in a Kolmogorov-Smirnov test to determine if the two ceramic styles present similar or different distribution patterns in the Province of Paruro. The results of the test rejected the null hypothesis (i.e., that there is no significant difference between the two samples) at a .05 level of confidence. In other words, the Kolmogorov-Smirnov test found a significant difference between the distribution patterns of Killke and Colcha pottery. This finding supports the suggestion that these two pottery styles are the products of two separate centers of ceramic production.

The suggestion that Killke and Colcha ceramics originated in two separate centers of pottery production can be further explored by comparing the density of sites containing these two ceramic styles in the survey region. A number of researchers have examined the distribution of various pottery styles from their centers of distribution or production, and various studies indicate that the spatial occurrence of pottery styles will frequently decline as a function of distance from their source (Hodder 1974; Hodder and Orton 1976; Renfew 1975; Orton 1980; Arnold 1980; Rice 1987:198–199).

The mathematical relationship between the density of sites containing Killke and Colcha pottery and their distance from Cuzco was examined in a series of regression analyses. If the production of Killke or Colcha pottery took place in the Cuzco Valley, then the density of sites with these ceramic styles should be greatest in the northern part of the survey region and should decrease as one moves farther south and the distance from Cuzco increases. The Killke pottery analysis indicates that the Yaurisque region contains the highest density of sites with Killke pottery (Fig. 11). This is the section of the survey area that is closest to Cuzco. The density of Killke sites drops steadily as the distance from Cuzco increases. Since the discovery of Killke pottery near Cuzco by Rowe in the early 1940s, it has been assumed that Killke ceramics were produced somewhere in the Cuzco Valley. The inverse relationship that appears to exist between the density of sites containing Killke pottery and their distance from Cuzco implies that the Cuzco Valley may indeed represent the production and distribution center of Killke pottery.

Colcha pottery, however, presents a very different distribution pattern from that of Killke pottery (Fig. 10). Although sites with Colcha pottery can be found in the northernmost reaches of the research area near the town of Yaurisque, as well as at the southern limits near the town of Accha, the density of sites with Colcha pottery is greatest near the community of Araypallpa. If the production of Colcha pot-

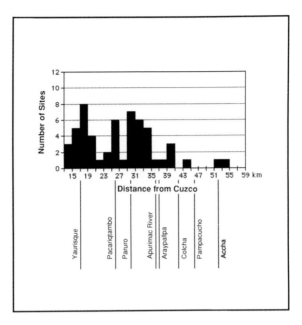

Figure 9. Distance of Sites with Killke Pottery from Cuzco

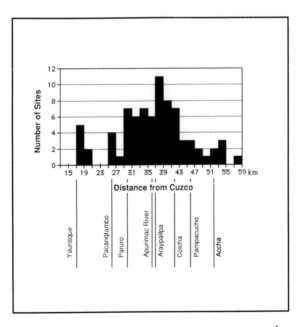

Figure 10. Distance of Sites with Colcha Pottery from Cuzco

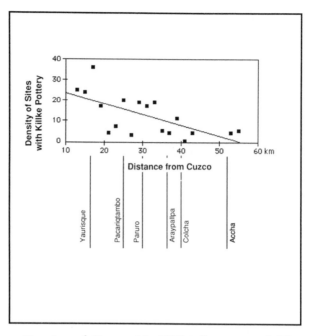

Figure 11. Density of Sites with Killke Pottery and Distance from Cuzco

tery took place in or near the village of Araypallpa, the density of sites containing this ceramic style should decrease as a function of distance from this suggested manufacturing locus. To test this hypothesis, the distance of sites containing Colcha pottery from the Araypallpa area was calculated and submitted to a regression analysis (Fig. 12). The results suggest that the density of sites that contain Colcha pottery declines rapidly as the distance from Araypallpa increases. These findings support the hypothesis that the Araypallpa area represented the center of Colcha pottery production and distribution during the Killke Period. As will be discussed below, ethnographic and historical evidence also supports this conclusion.

Ethnographic and Historical Information for Pottery Production in the Province of Paruro

Preliminary ethnographic data from the Province of Paruro indicate that the community of Araypallpa, located just south of the Apurimac River, is the only village in the region that has retained a tradition of pottery production.[12] Currently, the villagers of Araypallpa are best

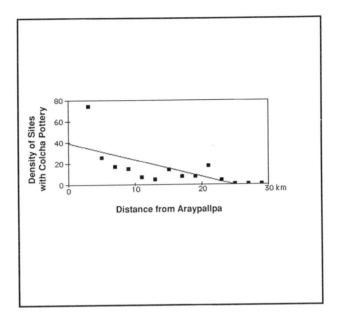

Figure 12. Density of Sites with Colcha Pottery and Distance from Araypallpa

known for their production of large, undecorated *chicha* (corn beer) fermentation jars that stand approximately 1 m high. These items, like other vessels manufactured in Araypallpa, are frequently called "Chillque."[13] Chicha vessels of this kind, manufactured in Araypallpa, were noted in every community within the research region. Villagers in communities as far away as Mollebamba and Yaurisque continue to describe these vessels as the preferred storage containers for chicha, and many informants remarked that their vessels were more than three generations old. In addition, older informants frequently recalled arduous two- to three-day journeys that they undertook as youths to transport these vessels from Araypallpa to their community. These ethnographic data, which indicate that the village of Araypallpa was a widely recognized regional center for ceramic manufacture until the middle of the twentieth century, support the suggestion that this village may also have been an important pottery production center in the more distant past.

Further evidence supporting the proposition that the villagers of Araypallpa were important potters before and during the Spanish Conquest is preserved in colonial documents. As was noted in Chapter 2, the name "Chillque" was applied to the group of Inca de Privilegio that occupied the region south of the Apurimac River during the Late Prehistoric and Early Historic periods. The center of this ethnic group was the community of Araypallpa (Poole 1984:468). The name "Chillque" is currently applied to the vessels that are manufactured in this same village. Thus there appears to be a recognizable link between the production of pottery in the area south of the Apurimac River and the Chillque Inca de Privilegio who inhabited that region. This link is made explicit by the indigenous chronicler Guamán Poma de Ayala in a description of the nature of various Inca de Privilegio in the Cuzco region:

> En la ley de los *Yngas* se ordenaua para ser rrey, *Capac Apo Ynga. Ynga* no quiere dezir dezir [sic] rrey cino que *ynga* ay gente uaja como *Chilque ynga* ollero; *Acos ynga* enbustero; *Uaroc ynga Llulla Uaroc* mentiroso . . . (Guamán Poma de Ayala [1615:117–118] 1980:96)

> In the law of the Inca they ordained "Capac Apo Inca" to be king. Inca does not mean king. Instead as Inca there are low-status people like Chillque Inca potter; Acos Inca cheater; Uaroc Inca Llulla Uaroc liar . . .

In sum, based on the preliminary results of pottery distribution studies in the Province of Paruro, and in light of ethnographic and historical data that complement the archaeological survey findings, there appears to be strong evidence to suggest that Araypallpa represents the center for Colcha pottery during the Killke Period.

Summary and Discussion

Archaeological investigations in the Province of Paruro have documented the widespread presence of Killke pottery and a new, Killke-related pottery style named "Colcha." The two pottery styles are stylistically similar, sharing a common repertoire of geometric design elements and vessel forms. They differ, however, in paste composition and slip type, as well as in some design motifs, colors, and application techniques.

Test excavations were conducted in the survey region to determine the chronological relationship between these two pottery styles. Test excavations at the site of Tejahuasi found both pottery styles in a sealed context, dating to A.D. 1010 ± 140. The recovery of both pottery styles within a single, undisturbed context provides conditional evidence to suggest that Killke and Colcha pottery were used contemporaneously.

Sites containing Killke pottery, as discussed above, are concentrated in the northern reaches of the study zone nearest Cuzco, and their numbers decrease as one moves southward. Killke pottery has, however, been found near the community of Araypallpa, in Chillque territory, as well as at the southern limits of the survey zone in the Accha region. It has also been noted that the presence of Colcha pottery decreases with distance from the village of Araypallpa. Examples of Colcha pottery have, nevertheless, been identified in our surface collections as far north as the Yaurisque River Valley and in the southern reaches of the survey zone in Accha.[14] Thus, from the archaeological survey data presented in this chapter, it is possible to conclude that Killke pottery may have been produced in the Cuzco Valley, and it appears likely, based on archaeological, ethnographic, and historical data, that Colcha pottery was manufactured by members of the Chillque ethnic group in the region of Araypallpa. However, the social mechanisms through which the pottery and/or the potters themselves[15] were traded or exchanged by the various ethnic groups discussed in this study remain to be investigated once further archaeological and historical work has been completed in the region.

Killke Period Ceramic Styles and Regional Ethnic Groups

Historical evidence suggests that the Cuzco Valley and the region immediately south of the valley were inhabited by at least four separate ethnic groups.[16] The Inca controlled the northern end of the Cuzco Valley. The Chillque occupied the region south of the Apurimac River near the present-day communities of Araypallpa and Colcha, and they may have controlled parts of Paruro and Ccochirhuay. The Masca and Tambo were located in the areas of Yaurisque and Pacariqtambo, between the Chillque to the south and the Inca to the north. The Masca were concentrated around Yaurisque and perhaps dominated areas as far south as Paruro and as far west as Huanoquite, while the Tambo appear to have been centered in and around the Pacariqtambo area (see Chapter 2).

The identification of two contemporaneous, regionally produced Killke Period ceramic styles in the area directly south of Cuzco raises an important question: Can the exact boundaries of the region's ethnic groups be identified through the distribution of these pottery styles? If the territorial boundaries of the Inca, Chillque, Masca, and Tambo were important factors in the distribution of Killke and Colcha pottery, then the density curves of the Killke and Colcha pottery types could be expected to display a series of "plateaus and kinks," reflecting the trade of ceramic vessels in and across ethnic territories (Hodder

1980:152). On the other hand, if the various ethnic boundaries of the region did not affect the distribution of Killke and/or Colcha ceramic materials, then the density of sites containing these ceramic types might simply decline as the distance from their sources of production increases. An analysis of preliminary archaeological survey data from the Province of Paruro indicates that the density of sites containing Killke and Colcha pottery styles displays relatively smooth and uninterrupted fall-off curves from their suggested centers of production. These findings suggest that both the Inca of the Cuzco Valley and the Chillque of the Araypallpa area primarily, although certainly not exclusively, used pottery produced within their own territory. The archaeological survey has recorded both Killke and Colcha ceramic styles distributed across the territories of the Masca and Tambo, and to a lesser extent each of these two styles appears to have entered into the other's region of production. The recovery of Killke and Colcha pottery in the territories of all four ethnic groups living in Cuzco and immediately to the south implies that the boundaries of these groups were not critical features in the distribution of Killke or Colcha pottery; archaeologically, ceramic styles in the Cuzco region do not appear to reflect elements from which ethnic identity might be inferred.

Killke Period Ceramic Styles and the Emergence of the Inca State

Although the distribution of Killke and Killke-related pottery styles south of Cuzco cannot be used to identify the boundaries of separate groups of Inca de Privilegio, their distribution patterns and methods of manufacture may provide important insights into the chronology and mode of state emergence in the Cuzco region. The use of nearly identical design elements and motifs in Killke and Killke-related pottery styles, such as the Colcha style, suggests that strong social contacts existed between the various centers of pottery production. In addition, the overlapping distribution networks of Colcha and Killke pottery imply that a high level of trade and exchange existed between various groups of Inca de Privilegio during the Killke Period. From these overlapping ceramic distribution patterns and their associated lines of communication, it may be tentatively proposed that the Killke Period in the Cuzco region was typified by regional accordance and exchange. Such a vision of regional unanimity stands in contrast to the general acceptance of a pre-Inca, or Killke, period marked with regional conflicts and competition and needs to be further investigated.

While Killke and Colcha pottery appear to be stylistically very similar and share overlapping distribution networks, the distribution ranges of the two pottery styles from their separate centers of production are markedly different. The distribution radius of Colcha pottery appears to be approximately 25 aerial kilometers from its area of production (Fig. 12). This is very limited when compared to the distribution radius of Killke pottery, which extends more than 60 aerial kilometers from the Cuzco Valley (Fig. 11). The greater distribution range of Killke pottery compared to that of Colcha pottery may be of some importance. From these observations it is possible to suggest that regional exchange relationships had already begun to develop a Cuzcocentric focus during the Killke Period and that the Cuzco Valley may have been emerging as a regional center of production during this same period.

Further evidence indicative of regional centralized authority developing in the Cuzco Valley during the Killke Period may be observed in the technological attributes of Killke pottery production. For example, Killke pottery is slightly more sophisticated in complexity of decoration and in ware than other Cuzco regional styles. In addition, the widespread distribution of Killke pottery suggests that it was produced in far greater quantities than any other Killke-related style. The emergence of what appears to be large-scale craft production in the Cuzco Valley may reflect the development of full-time specialists in ceramic production during the Killke Period. While superior quality and greater quantities of craft production do not necessarily indicate that a high level of sociopolitical organization existed in the Cuzco Valley, when this evidence is combined with the distribution information of Killke pottery it suggests that the Cuzco Valley was a regional center for exchange, and perhaps authority, by the Killke Period.

The ceramic distribution patterns south of Cuzco may show further evidence of regional exchange relationships during the Killke Period that is indicative of the unification of the region under a single, Cuzco-based political authority. Systematic regional surveys conducted in Accha, 52 aerial kilometers from Cuzco, revealed a light presence of Killke pottery. Four days of survey work in the more southern region of Omacha, approximately 70 aerial kilometers from Cuzco, found no evidence of Killke pottery, suggesting that the area between Accha and Omacha forms the frontier for Killke pottery distribution to the south of Cuzco. The chronicles suggest that this same region also represented the outer limits of the Inca de Privilegio. The apparent correlation between the distribution of Killke pottery and the distribution of groups absorbed into the Inca state as Inca de Privilegio indicates that Cuzcocentric distribution networks may have united Cuzco with surrounding ethnic groups during the period of state development.

If Cuzco emerged during the Killke Period as a dominant power in the region, with a level of social and political organization unsurpassed by other regional ethnic groups, it is possible that its elevated status might be reflected in various pottery designs produced by the Inca. There is provisional evidence to suggest that this may have occurred. In the Killke ceramic tradition, a highly stylized figure is frequently depicted on the single-handled jars (Fig. 13).[17] This figure can be identified through a set of standardized motifs, including (1) a headdress or cap *(chullo)* depicted by a series of wide, evenly spaced bands, outlined on each side by two to three narrow lines, that is located on the vessel's rim and upper border section; (2) a headband motif that is most frequently depicted as a row of nested triangles; and (3) a series of linked diamonds or triangles on the figure's cheeks. The human qualities of the figure stand in contrast to the pantheon of mythoreligious figures represented in earlier ceramic traditions, such as Huari, that have been found in the Cuzco region (McEwan 1987). The standardized headdress, the elaborate headband, and the painted cheeks are suggestive of emblems of power and authority. The appearance of this stylized figure during the Killke Period and the conspicuous absence of other figures on Killke pottery vessels suggest that it may be a symbolic representation of an institutionalized ruler or elite class. The appearance of this figure on pottery thought to have been manufactured in the Cuzco Valley hints at the possibility that the institution of the "Inca" as a paramount ruler or a dominant social class had begun to coalesce by the Killke Period. Although the very suggestion that certain pottery designs may in some way be reflective of the sociopolitical order that produced them is extremely speculative, the appearance of this kinglike figure on Killke pottery during the period of early state development does concur with other preliminary conclusions drawn from the ceramic distribution data.

Under the traditional model of state formation in the Cuzco region, presented by the Spanish chronicles and accepted by many Andean ethnohistorians and archaeologists, the Killke Period is characterized as a period of fierce regional conflict, a volatile world of raids, competing polities, and political fragmentation. The traditional model suggests that political and economic unity was achieved in the Cuzco region only after Pachacuti Inca Yupanqui's victory in the mythohistorical Chanca war. The archaeological evidence presented in this chapter concerning the production of pottery in the Province of Paruro during the Killke Period does not, however, conform to our expectations of a fragmentary and competing social landscape. It is suggested that, instead of being a time of regional conflict, the Killke Period was characterized by widespread regional exchange. Rather than

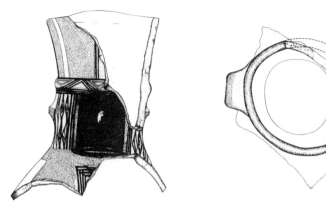

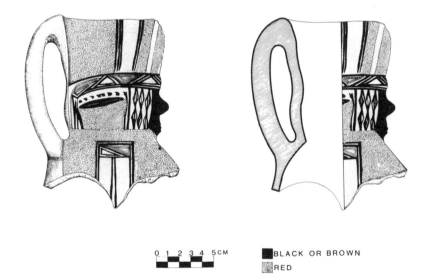

0 1 2 3 4 5CM

■ BLACK OR BROWN
▨ RED

Figure 13. Killke Face Neck Jar Fragment

competing with other ethnic groups, the Inca may have already dominated the local social and political organizations of the region. In addition, the Inca may have unified the Cuzco area and Cuzco may have already become the center of economic, and perhaps political, influence during this same period. In other words, it is possible that unification of the Cuzco region did not simply occur during the Killke Period, but came about specifically under Inca dominance. In addition, it is possible that during this period the hierarchical relationships that the rulers of Cuzco would hold over the members of other regional ethnic groups at the time of the Spanish Conquest were in formation, or were already present.

6.

The Subsistence-Settlement Systems of the Province of Paruro during the Killke and Inca Periods

THE PURPOSE OF THIS CHAPTER is to compare the Killke Period subsistence-settlement systems of the Province of Paruro to those of the Inca Period. The study is conducted to gain information on the social and economic conditions south of Cuzco during the period of state development. In the first section of the chapter, the previous settlement studies of the Cuzco region are reviewed. The findings of these studies support the traditional, or event-based, model of state development, namely that the Killke Period was characterized by warring polities and that a radical reorganization of the Cuzco region occurred during the Inca Period under the leadership of Pachacuti Inca Yupanqui. In the second section of the chapter, the Killke and Inca period subsistence-settlement systems of the ethnic groups living in the Province of Paruro are examined. By comparing the Killke Period subsistence-settlement systems of the region before the development of the Inca state with those of the Inca Period, two general research issues may be addressed: (1) How were the inhabitants south of Cuzco spatially reorganized during the assimilation of the region into the Inca state? and (2) What are the economic implications of the reorganization? In the third section, the results of the subsistence-settlement studies conducted in the Province of Paruro will be compared with the findings of other projects in the Cuzco region and elsewhere in the Andes.

Previous Killke Period Settlement Studies in the Cuzco Region

The Spanish chronicles suggest that the Cuzco region was formally composed of a number of warring ethnic groups (Sarmiento de Gamboa [1572, Chap. 24] 1906; Betanzos [1551, Chap. 16] 1987). The Inca of this volatile prestate period are traditionally portrayed as one of a number of small-scale rural societies that were involved in constant raids against other ethnic groups of the region (Rowe 1946:203; Brundage 1963:13; Conrad and Demarest 1984:96, 106). The chronicles suggest that just before the Chanca war, the balance of power in the Cuzco region began to sway in favor of the Inca, as Viracocha Inca initiated a series of bold conquests to subdue nearby ethnic groups:

> Subjetó los pueblos que hay desde el Cuzco hasta Quiquixana, y sus alrededores, y los Papres, y otros pueblos en su contorno, todos en siete y ocho leguas á lo más á la redonda del Cuzco. En las cuales conquistas hizo grandísimas crueldades, robos, muertes, destruiciones de pueblos, quemándolos y asolándolos por los caminos sin dejar memoria de algunos dellos. (Sarmiento de Gamboa [1572, Chap. 25] 1906:58)

> The Inca subjugated the towns from Cuzco to Quiquixana, and their surroundings, and the Papres, and other towns in their environs, all seven or eight leagues at the most from Cuzco. In these conquests the Inca committed great cruelties, robberies, murders, and destruction of towns, burning and razing them along the roads without leaving any memory of them.

After the Cuzco victory over the Chanca, the conquest and reorganization of the Cuzco region by the Inca was, according to the chronicles, vigorously expanded by Pachacuti Inca Yupanqui. Rowe summarizes information collected from a number of different Spanish chronicles concerning the military campaigns of the Inca in the Cuzco region under the rule of Pachacuti Inca Yupanqui: "The *Inca* conquests started with a campaign in the lower Urubamba Valley and in Vilcapampa which Pachacuti undertook immediately after his victory over the *Chanca* (Cobo, 1890–95, bk. 12, ch. 12; Sarmiento, 1906, chs. 33–35). Having consolidated his power at home, he turned west through the *Quechua* and *Chanca* country, and conquered Soras and Vilcas. From Soras he sent General Capac Yupanqui to reconnoiter the south coast, and then occupied Aymaraes, Omasayos, Cotapampas and Chilques" (Rowe 1946:206).

Many researchers have accepted such literal readings of the chronicles as accurate descriptions of the past, and previous archaeological work in the Cuzco region has been used to support the chronicles' claims of Pachacuti Inca Yupanqui's heroic leadership. For example, after the military defeat of the Cuzco ethnic groups, Pachacuti Inca Yupanqui is said to have moved the settlements of these groups from fortified sites to newly created, unfortified locations. Rowe (1944:61, 1957; 1970:557) believes that he has found evidence of such a movement in the Chita area immediately north of the Cuzco Valley: "Here we found a hill-top site [Muyu-muyu (Moyo-moyo, Ck. 7)] with rough terracing and some attempt at fortification, where Killke types were abundant and pure. At the foot of the hill was another site (Arayañni-yoq, Ck. 6) with pure Cuzco Series sherds, and cut-stone blocks of characteristic Late Inca style. These two sites seem to reflect the Inca policy begun by Inca Pachacuti of moving conquered villages down from their old hill-forts to new towns on the level" (Rowe 1944:61).

Additional information concerning the location of Killke Period sites in the Cuzco region is presented in Dwyer's 1971 study of Killke pottery. After completing an informal survey of the Cuzco Valley, Dwyer concluded that none of the sites in the valley contained defensive works dating to the Killke Period (1971:145). Dwyer found that, rather than being surrounded by fortification walls or situated on defensible ridges, the Killke Period sites in the Cuzco Valley were unfortified and generally located on or adjacent to the valley floor.

The findings of Dwyer's survey conflicted with what little information was available at the time on Killke Period sites outside of the Cuzco Valley. Earlier explorations outside of the Valley of Cuzco, especially to the north, implied that most Killke Period sites were located on hilltops or steep ridges and contained defensive features (Dwyer 1971:146). Dwyer reconciled his observations on the unfortified Killke Period sites near Cuzco with reports of fortified Killke Period sites outside the valley by concluding that the immediate pre–Inca Period was, as reported by the Spanish chronicles, a time of regional warfare. However, according to Dwyer, this warfare occurred on the perimeters of the Cuzco Valley rather than within it:

> Outside of the valley of Cuzco, all Killke sites so far reported are located in easily defensible positions. They are usually on the tops of high ridges at some distance from good agricultural land. The exact function of these fortresses has not yet been clearly demonstrated. They may have been seasonally occupied, or they may have only been used during times of stress as retreats, like castles in the medieval sense. It is possible, but not likely, that they were continuously occupied. In considering this type of site the most interesting factor is its almost ubiquitous occurrence outside of the valley of Cuzco contrasted with its absence within the valley. There was no place for the inhabitants of Cuzco to retreat to in times of crisis. This almost suggests that Cuzco was an oasis of tranquillity surrounded by a disturbed and ravaged buffer zone. (Dwyer 1971:146)

In summary, previous archaeological work in the Cuzco region has been used to support the traditional, or event-based, model of Inca state growth. Under this model, the perceived sudden development of the Inca state and the conquest of the Cuzco region by the Inca brought radical social and economic changes to the area. Local ethnic groups that once rivaled the Inca for power were subdued and the local settlement systems of the Cuzco region were reorganized to benefit the ruling Inca. This brief period of state formation in the Cuzco region was completed, according to the chronicles, with the abandonment of fortified sites and the relocation of the regional groups into new villages constructed by or under the direction of the Inca.

Killke and Inca Period Subsistence-Settlement Systems in the Province of Paruro

Using information gathered in the archaeological survey of the Province of Paruro, a number of important questions can be posed concerning the prestate social and economic organizations of the Cuzco region and the effect that state growth had on these organizations. For example, the traditional model of Inca state formation suggests that the Killke Period was a time of intense regional conflict. Is there evidence of fortification in the Province of Paruro that would support the notion that the Killke Period was characterized by regional warfare? In addition, the traditional model of state growth suggests that Pachacuti Inca Yupanqui reorganized the local economies of the Cuzco region and forcibly resettled many of the ethnic groups. Are there changes in site location between the Killke Period settlements and those of the Inca Period that would indicate changes in resource exploitation patterns? Is an Inca policy of resettlement reflected in the abandonment of Killke Period village sites and the creation of new Inca sites?

The four areas of the research region located closest to the Cuzco Valley—Pacariqtambo, Yaurisque, Paruro, and Colcha—were selected for intensive study to begin to answer the above questions.[1] The ecology of the Province of Paruro and the survey methodology used during the course of the fieldwork have been described in Chapter 4. Site size estimates were established from aerial photographs or, in the case of the smallest sites, from measurements taken while conducting the survey. At most sites, it was not possible to estimate the relative area covered by each temporal component. Like other regional settlement studies in the central Andes (Earle et al. 1980, 1988; D'Altroy 1981; Parsons and Hastings 1977), it has been assumed in this study that each component at a site covered the site's entire area (LeBlanc 1981:239).

In the following discussion, the prehistoric occupations of the Province of Paruro are classified into three general size groups: (1) small sites (<1 hectare), (2) hamlets or small villages (>1 hectare and <5 hectares), and (3) regional state installations (>5 hectares). The smaller sites frequently measure from 25 m to 50 m in diameter. These sites, based on ethnographic analogies, are thought to be the remains of isolated dwellings and/or seasonally occupied residences. The medium-sized settlements appear to represent the permanent rural occupations of the region, while the site of Maukallaqta (the only site of the research region in the large-site-size category) is categorized as a major Inca state facility.

Analysis of Site Size Frequencies

During the survey of the Pacariqtambo, Yaurisque, Paruro, and Colcha areas, eighty-five Killke Period sites were identified. Of these sites, forty-seven are relatively small, measuring less than 1 hectare, with the other thirty-eight sites measuring between 1.0 and 3.5 hectares in size (Fig. 14A). None of the Killke Period sites contain any obvious evidence of fortification. Several sites are located on narrow ridges; however, this occurs in the more remote parts of the region, where ridgetops provide the only flat areas for settlement.

Within the four areas selected for intensive investigation, 131 Inca Period sites were also identified. These sites varied greatly in size, from small concentrations of pottery with no visible architectural remains to Maukallaqta, which measures nearly 6 hectares. Approximately 70 percent (89 by number) of the Inca Period sites in the region are small scatters of pottery (Fig. 14B). The other 30 percent of the sites in the region are represented by a continuum of settlements that range from 1.0 to 3.5 hectares in size, and by the large site of Maukallaqta.

The Killke and Inca period site size frequencies are similar (Fig. 14); however, they are not identical. The simple two-step settlement size hierarchy (i.e., isolated structures and small village occupations) among the Killke Period sites suggests that a decentralized form of economic and political organization existed among the Chillque, Masca, and Tambo ethnic groups. The Inca Period, and the subsequent construction of Maukallaqta, brought an important new dimension to this regional settlement size hierarchy. The disproportional size of Maukallaqta, dwarfing all other sites in the area, and its fine Inca stone masonry, unmatched in any other site in the Province of Paruro, suggest that Maukallaqta was a state installation of considerable importance imposed by the Inca on the various Inca de Privilegio groups south of Cuzco. The construction of a large state facility south

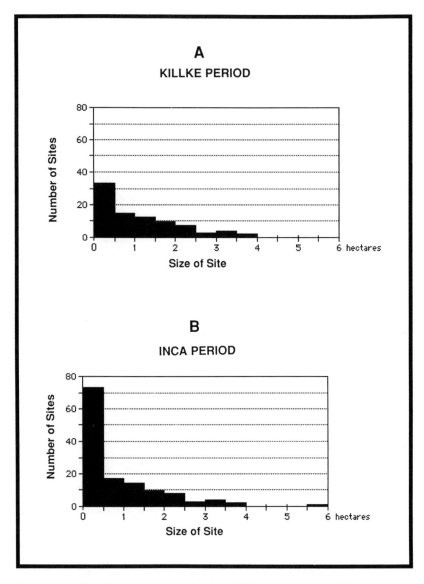

Figure 14. Site Size Frequency for (A) Killke Period and (B) Inca Period Sites in the Region of Pacariqtambo, Yaurisque, Paruro, and Colcha

of Cuzco added an additional third step to the regional site hierarchy. The shift from a bimodal to a trimodal settlement size curve in the Province of Paruro between the Killke and Inca periods most likely reflects the development of a strongly ranked society in the Cuzco region from the more egalitarian polities of the previous era (Wright and Johnson 1975; Isbell and Schreiber 1978).

Analysis of Site Sizes and Elevations

The ethnohistorian John Murra (1972) has suggested that most prehistoric Andean polities preferred direct access to resources from different ecological zones, rather than relying on extensive trade networks between zones. Murra's model of vertical control or vertical economies specifically suggests that in regions of steep mountain gradients and closely spaced ecological zones, such as those found in the Province of Paruro, the pre-Hispanic Andean communities strove toward self-sufficiency through the simultaneous exploitation of a number of different zones.[2] The Killke and Inca period settlement data from the Province of Paruro displayed in Figure 15 concur with Murra's model of vertical economies.

Figure 15 shows a widespread distribution of small Killke and Inca period sites between the elevations of 2,850 and 4,000 masl.[3] The distribution of these small sites across the four ecological zones of the region and their lack of visible architectural remains suggest that the majority of the sites represent isolated, seasonally occupied dwellings related to specialized exploitation activities. The modern analogues to these sites are the many *estancias* (remote dwellings) of the region, which are occupied during the agricultural season and are left abandoned the rest of the year. A light scatter of Killke and Inca pottery found near the summit of Cerro Masca at 4,300 masl and two small scatters of Inca pottery found adjacent to the highest mountain peaks of the region, Cerro Pumawasi and Cerro Imanco, are also noted on Figure 15. As these sites are located on important mountains well above the effective limits of agricultural production, they may be related to the role of the mountain peaks as major apus of the region.

The larger Killke and Inca period sites of the Province of Paruro, in contrast to the smaller sites, are closely distributed between 3,100 and 3,750 masl. The majority of the larger Killke and Inca period sites are situated on small knolls or lower valley slopes. The locations of these sites offer particular advantages; the inhabitants of the area had direct access to the rich river valley bottomlands, while the settlements themselves occupied the less productive lands of the region. The location of these village settlements suggests that the cultivation of maize

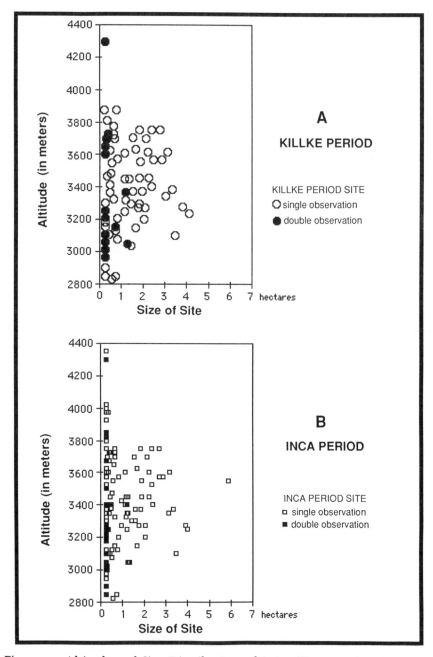

Figure 15. Altitude and Size Distribution of (A) Killke Period and (B) Inca Period Sites in the Region of Pacariqtambo, Yaurisque, Paruro, and Colcha

and other grain cultigens, such as quinoa, represented a primary agricultural focus for the inhabitants of the Province of Paruro. At the same time, however, it is evident that the full range of ecological zones and products of the region (particularly potatoes) was being exploited through a series of small sites located at a distance from the larger permanent settlements. The relatively small sizes of the permanent settlements in the Pacariqtambo, Yaurisque, Paruro, and Colcha areas also indicate that the ethnic groups of the region lived in hamlets or villages, rather than in large, nucleated sociopolitical centers. Evidence will be presented in Chapter 8 suggesting that many of these villages were occupied by single kinship groups, or ayllus, and that although they were physically separate and economically self-sufficient, the settlements were united through moiety systems.

Comparison of the Killke and Inca period occupations, as displayed in Figure 15, provides additional information on the late prehistoric subsistence-settlement systems for the area south of Cuzco. The scattergrams show that all the village settlements (>1 hectare) occupied during the Killke Period continued to be occupied during the Inca Period. The only Killke Period sites that appear to have been abandoned before the Inca Period are eight small sites (<1 hectare), which, based on their limited size and material remains, do not appear to represent major loci of occupation. Since all of the Killke Period village sites were also occupied in the Inca Period, there is no archaeological evidence to support the notion that a large number of Killke Period sites were abandoned with the advent of the Inca state.

There are, however, seven medium-to-large Inca Period sites (>1 hectare) in the region that showed no surface evidence of Killke Period remains. The first of these sites is the Inca ruin of Maukallaqta. No clear Killke or Killke-related materials were found in limited surface collections or test excavations conducted at the site. Another important site of the region that yielded no evidence of Killke Period material is the rock outcrop of Puma Orco. However, this site, like Maukallaqta, produced an extremely small collection of surface pottery.[4] Five other medium-sized sites (two near Pacariqtambo and three near Paruro) contained no surface evidence of Killke Period remains. These sites are represented by pottery scatters (each measuring just over 1 hectare) located in open, recently plowed agricultural land with good ground visibility. The absence of Killke Period pottery at these sites suggests that they may represent sites built after the development of the Inca state.

The scattergrams also reveal that there are a greater number of small sites in the Inca Period than in the Killke Period. Archaeological surveys in the Pacariqtambo, Yaurisque, Paruro, and Colcha areas have found the remains of forty-seven small Killke Period sites and eighty-nine small Inca Period sites. One explanation for the observed difference is that the Killke Period subsistence-settlement system south of Cuzco required fewer short-term occupation sites. This would suggest that the various ecological zones of the region were being worked less intensively during the Killke Period than in the Inca Period. An increase in the number of short-term occupations between the Killke and Inca periods might reflect increased production requirements placed on the rural population by the Inca state or might stem from the increased supplementary needs of a growing population.

An alternative explanation is that the greater number of small Inca Period sites reflects preservation factors, rather than differences in resource exploitation patterns. By their very nature, isolated homesteads and seasonal occupations leave only ephemeral evidence in the archaeological record, and the combined forces of erosion and plowing can quickly destroy the remains of these small occupations. Thus, the relatively low number of small Killke Period sites identified in the Province of Paruro may simply be a result of poor preservation.

Summary and Discussion

Currently, little archaeological information exists on the economic organization of the Cuzco region either prior to, or during, the period of Inca rule. As a result, basic questions remain concerning the economic organization of the Inca de Privilegio groups and the changes that occurred in the Cuzco region as a result of state growth. This chapter has begun to address these concerns by examining the subsistence-settlement systems adopted by the Masca, Chillque, and Tambo during the Killke and Inca periods.

Data from the Province of Paruro suggest that the major population loci immediately south of Cuzco during the Killke and Inca periods were semiautonomous villages located in the midlevel ecological zones. Numerous smaller sites, spread between the altitudes of 2,850 and 4,000 masl, are thought to mark the locations of isolated and/or seasonal occupations used during the harvest of various crops or the pasturing of animals. The widespread presence of these small sites may indicate that self-sufficiency was achieved by the inhabitants of the region during both periods through the simultaneous exploitation of a number of different ecological zones. Several small sites have also been identified in altitudes over 4,300 masl near mountain summits. It is proposed that these sites are related to the role of these particular mountain peaks as apus.

The Spanish chronicles describe the immediate pre-Inca period in the Cuzco area as a time of intense regional warfare. They also suggest that a massive restructuring of the social and economic organization of the Cuzco region took place during or at the end of this period. Many traditional village sites are thought to have been abandoned as the Inca implemented a policy of forced resettlement of various ethnic groups. The Killke and Inca period subsistence-settlement data from south of Cuzco have, accordingly, been examined for evidence of intense regional conflict, as reflected by the presence of fortified sites. The survey data from the Province of Paruro have also been examined for possible indications of a large-scale Killke Period site abandonment episode and for evidence of the construction of new settlements in the region with the development of the Inca state. The results of these studies are markedly different from those implied by the Spanish chronicles. None of the Killke Period sites in the Province of Paruro contain any remains of fortifications. Indeed, rather than demonstrating that the ethnic groups of the area were concentrated in fortified communities, the data indicate that the various groups south of Cuzco may have occupied small, widely scattered, and unfortified villages or hamlets. In addition, since the vast majority of the Killke Period village sites of the region continued to be occupied into the Inca Period, there is currently little evidence indicating that the Inca implemented a resettlement policy south of Cuzco during the process of state growth. There are also few data that would suggest that numerous new settlements were established in the region with the advent of the Inca state. The only major addition to the subsistence-settlement system of the research region between the Killke and Inca periods appears to be the construction Maukallaqta, to the north of the modern-day town of Pacariqtambo.

As noted earlier in this chapter, Dwyer (1971) found that few of the Killke Period sites in the Cuzco Valley contain defensive structures and that most are located on or near the valley floor. The contrast between his study and preliminary reports of fortified Killke Period sites north of Cuzco led Dwyer (1971:146) to propose that during the Killke Period the Valley of Cuzco may have been ". . . an oasis of tranquillity surrounded by a disturbed and ravaged buffer zone." The results of our surveys south of Cuzco indicate that the Cuzco Valley may not be the exception it was once thought to be, and that the unanimity of the Killke Period may well have extended beyond the confines of the Cuzco Valley into the Province of Paruro.

In this respect it is interesting to note that many other regions of the Andes do contain clear evidence of chronic warfare during the immediate pre–Inca period.[5] For example, the Lake Titicaca region is said to have suffered under a nearly constant struggle between the Lupaca and the Colla. Numerous fortified hilltop sites on the shore of Lake Titicaca stand as monuments to the endemic prehistoric warfare of the region. Perhaps the largest of these fortified hilltop sites is Pucara Juli. This site is surrounded by no fewer than five large fortification walls, totaling more than 16 km in length (Hyslop 1976, 1990; Stanish n.d.). All of the hilltop sites of the region appear to have been abandoned as a result of the conquest of the area by the Inca (Stanish n.d.).

Archaeological remains suggest that a similar situation of chronic pre-Inca warfare existed in the Xauxa region. According to survey work by Parsons and Hastings (1977) and the archaeological investigations conducted by the Upper Mantaro Archaeological Research Project (Earle et al. 1980, 1988), the Xauxa region was controlled by several large, mutually hostile polities before the conquest of the region by the Inca. Extensive fortification walls are present at several pre-Inca sites in the region and other sites are located on high defensible hilltops or ridges (Earle et al. 1980:21). The conquest of the Mantaro region by the Inca brought dramatic social and economic changes to the area. The Inca completely reorganized the Xauxa territory, shifting the local population from large, nucleated settlements located in the potato production zones of the area to new, smaller settlements in the lower maize production zones (D'Altroy 1981; LeBlanc 1981; Hastorf 1983).

Preliminary information on Killke Period sites to the west and north of the Cuzco Valley can also be used, along with information from sites in the Province of Paruro, to assess the image of a war-torn Cuzco region, conquered and unified by Pachacuti Inca Yupanqui after the mythohistorical Chanca war. Heffernan (1989) has recently completed intensive exploration work in the Limatambo area, approximately 50 km west of Cuzco. His field observations and conclusions regarding the Killke Period settlements of this region are remarkably similar to those made in the Province of Paruro.[6] He finds that most of the Killke Period sites are located near large cultivable areas and that few if any of these sites contain clear evidence of fortification. In addition, he notes that while there may have been a small shift in population from higher to lower altitudes between the Killke and Inca periods in the Limatambo region, the overall subsistence-settlement patterns of these two periods are very similar. Comparing his field observations with information presented in the Spanish chronicles, Heffernan (1989:413) writes, "The mythico-historic characterization of pre-Inca populations as constantly warring, in light of field evidence, is imbalanced and fails to appreciate stable elements in the socio-economic landscape of Limatambo." Although systematic regional surveys have not been conducted elsewhere in the Cuzco region and many areas remain relatively unknown, there is currently only one clear case of a Killke Period fortified site in the Cuzco region. This is the site of Huata, located approximately 40 aerial kilometers northeast of Cuzco on a remote mountain summit, which is surrounded by three concentric fortification walls (MacCurdy 1923:225–227, Plate 14; Rowe 1944:53; Kendall 1985:321–325, Plan 10, Plates 32, 33).

Reconnaissance work done by Kendall (1974, 1976, 1985) in the Cusichaca River Valley, beyond Huata, also implies that a settlement pattern different from the ones documented for the Cuzco Valley, the Province of Paruro, and the Limatambo area may have existed in the far northern parts of the Cuzco region. The Cusichaca area, located approximately 70 aerial kilometers from Cuzco, between Ollantaytambo and Machu Picchu, falls just outside the region of Inca de Privilegio. Kendall (1974, 1976, 1985) reports that the Late Intermediate (or Killke Period) sites of the Cusichaca region, although not surrounded by fortification walls, are frequently located on extremely steep ridgetops. The presence of Killke Period ridgetop sites in the Cusichaca region, as well as at the fortified site of Huata, suggests that the northern edge of the Cuzco region, unlike the Cuzco Valley, the Paruro area, and the Limatambo region, may have seen regional hostilities before the Inca Period.

In summary, although evidence from other highland areas of Peru indicates that chronic warfare can leave evidence in the archaeological record, a survey of 600 km² directly south of Cuzco found no clear evidence of it. Our research found no defensive walls or other fortifications associated with any Killke Period sites in the Province of Paruro, and few occupations of this period were even found to be located in defensible positions. Instead, the majority of the Killke Period sites south of Cuzco are located on small knolls or on valley slopes adjacent to agricultural land. In addition, the absorption of the Province of Paruro into the developing Inca state appears to have left the subsistence-settlement system of the region largely unaltered. At this stage of research, there is little evidence of the massive site abandonment mentioned in the chronicles or of a large-scale reorganization of the general subsistence-settlement system by the Inca.

This is not to imply, however, that there was a complete absence of competition or conflict among the ethnic groups of the Cuzco region during the Killke or Inca periods. It should be noted that there are numerous historical references to *tinkuys* (ritual battles) taking place in the Cuzco region at the time of Spanish contact. In addition, it is possible that hostilities were vented in skirmishes that took place in open territory and therefore did not require the construction of fortified sites. Nevertheless, it can be noted that the survey data from the Province of Paruro are clearly different from data collected in other regions of the Andes, such as Lake Titicaca and Xauxa. From the valley bottom locations of many Killke Period villages and the apparent lack of Killke Period fortified sites in the Province of Paruro, it is possible to suggest that the animosities between the Cuzco Valley and regions to the south were of a limited nature and that the Killke Period in the Cuzco region should not necessarily be characterized as a time of chronic regional warfare.

After an analysis of the ceramic distribution patterns south of Cuzco in Chapter 5, it was proposed that the Inca may have reached a level of sociopolitical organization during the Killke Period that enabled them to unify or politically dominate the Province of Paruro. A preliminary examination of the subsistence-settlement data from south of Cuzco supports this suggestion. The scarcity of fortified sites in the region of investigation and the continuous subsistence-settlement systems from the Killke and Inca periods—interpreted as reflecting a relatively unbelligerent transition between these two periods—suggest that the Province of Paruro may have been part of the original core area of state formation or that the region was absorbed into the Inca state through nonmilitary means.

7.

Maukallaqta and Puma Orco

REGIONAL ARCHAEOLOGICAL STUDIES are based on the premise that no single site is representative of a prehistoric society as a whole (Hutterer and Macdonald 1982:162). The analyses in this work have been conducted within a regional framework that examines the range and distribution patterns of late-prehistoric remains in the Province of Paruro for evidence of state growth. In Chapter 5, the regional exchange networks south of Cuzco, as reflected in the distribution of Killke and Colcha pottery, and their significance for state development were discussed. In Chapter 6, the Killke and Inca period subsistence-settlement systems of the survey region were investigated, and in Chapter 8, the Killke and Inca period moiety organizations of Pacariqtambo will be examined. Through these comparisons, this work has begun to analyze the economic and social organizations of the ethnic groups south of Cuzco during their assimilation into the Inca state.

Even within a regional research framework, however, there are certain sites that, due to unusual features, demand special consideration and detailed discussions. Maukallaqta (Old City) and Puma Orco (Puma Mountain) in the Province of Paruro are two such sites. As discussed earlier, the large size of Maukallaqta distinguishes it from the other Inca Period occupations in the survey region and adds an important new dimension to the site hierarchy of the region. Other distinguishing features of Maukallaqta are the orderly layout of the buildings, the presence of very fine stone architecture (Plates 6 and 7), and a central court. Puma Orco, a nearby rock outcrop, is distinguished by elaborately carved boulders at its base and a carved summit. Since these sites represent the largest, most elaborate, and arguably the most important Inca state installations in the region, no study of the late pre-Hispanic archaeological remains in the Province of Paruro would

Plate 6. One of Several Large Gateways at Maukallaqta

Plate 7. Example of Very Fine Inca Stonework at Maukallaqta

be complete without a discussion of them. Accordingly, it is the purpose of this brief chapter to discuss the site of Maukallaqta, and to a
lesser extent Puma Orco, in an effort to evaluate the roles they may
have held in governing the Inca de Privilegio of the Province of Paruro
and to evaluate, if possible, their importance during the process of
Inca state growth.[1]

Maukallaqta

Maukallaqta comprises the ruins of more than 200 structures. It is situated on a wide, slightly curving mountain shelf on the western side
of the Huaynacancha Quebrada, a small tributary of the Yaurisque
River. The ruins are spread across the mountain shelf in seven zones
(Fig. 16). Four of the zones are naturally defined by dry quebradas, and
three have been distinguished by architectural differences. All of the
buildings of the site are aligned along grid systems established within
each zone (see Bauer 1990a, 1992, for additional plans of the site).

The most impressive feature of the ruins of Maukallaqta is the central court of zone 1 (Fig. 16). This court of fine Inca stone masonry
measures approximately 13.5 m across and is laid out on a north-south
alignment. Each of its three sides appears to contain three large triple-
jamb niches, each measuring approximately 2.8 m at the base and
more than 1 m deep (Plate 8). Although it is difficult to determine their
height because of poor adobe preservation, the niches would have
measured more than 3 m high.

While each of the nine niches is striking, the central one on the
north wall deserves special attention (Plate 9). Unlike the other eight
niches in the central court, this one is not properly a niche, since it
has no back wall, but rather a niche entrance, which provides access
to a passageway leading into an inner chamber of the court. In contrast to the rest of the single-room structures at Maukallaqta and to
Inca architecture in general, this inner chamber is composed of four
adjacent rooms in a line with a smaller connecting room off its southwest corner.

The central court of Maukallaqta includes an outer chamber as well,
to the east of and sharing a wall with the inner chamber. The outer
chamber consists of two rooms and a small side room, also off its
southwest corner. In comparison with the niche entrance to the inner
chamber, the outer chamber's doorway is large and occupies a com-
manding position within the central court and the layout of the ruins.
The two chambers share a common inner wall and are connected by
three small windows. As will be discussed later in this chapter, the unusual court area of Maukallaqta and its two adjacent chambers may be

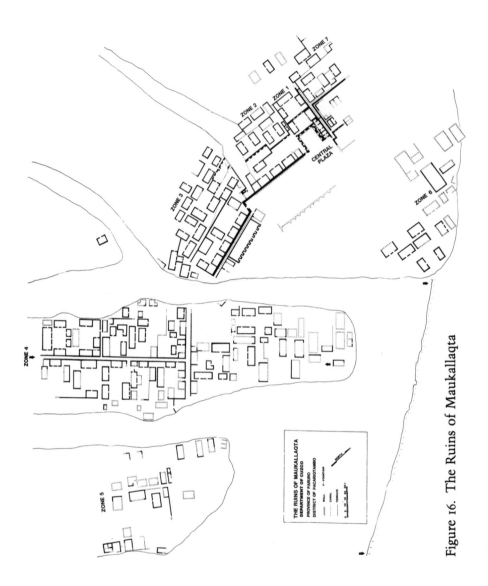

Figure 16. The Ruins of Maukallaqta

Plate 8. West Wall of Maukallaqta's Central Court (Reprinted by permission of the Society for American Archaeology from Bauer 1991a: Figure 10.)

Plate 9. Central Niche of the North Wall of Maukallaqta's Central Court (Reprinted by permission of the Society for American Archaeology from Bauer 1991a: Figure 11.)

of critical importance in determining the role this Inca installation held in the governance of the Cuzco region.

Puma Orco

Looking east from the ruins of Maukallaqta across the Huaynacancha Quebrada, one sees Puma Orco (Plates 10 and 11).[2] This massive stone outcrop, with a rock fall at its northern end, towers above the surrounding river valley on a small spur of land beside the Huaynacancha River.

There is a cave, formed by the superposition of several boulders, at the northern base of Puma Orco. The cave is approximately 6 m wide, 4 m high, and 4 m deep. A passageway leads into the northern rock fall area between the boulders that make up one side of this cave and the vertical face of Puma Orco. There are a number of carved boulders in the rock fall area. On the eastern side of Puma Orco are the remains of three small, poorly preserved Inca buildings, a carved outcrop, and a series of terraces leading down to the small Huaynacancha River. The summit of Puma Orco was completely transformed by Inca carvers into a continuous series of horizontal and vertical planes, and at the highest point are the vandalized remains of two carved pumas. Settings for stone blocks run along the outer edge of the summit, indicating that it was circumscribed by a stone wall. Surface collections at the rock outcrop of Puma Orco were not sufficient to date the site, but the carvings at its base and summit and the buildings along its eastern side appear to date to the Inca Period.[3] It will be argued at the end of this chapter that this outcrop and the site of Maukallaqta may represent the location where the Inca believed their first mythical king, Manco Capac, emerged from the earth; as such, the function of these sites may have been unique.

Recent Archaeological Research at Maukallaqta and Puma Orco

Surface collections were conducted at the sites of Maukallaqta and Puma Orco in 1984.[4] However, due to the thick grass cover and slope wash at both of these locations, only a few fragments were found. An additional collection was made at Maukallaqta in 1986, on the lower slopes of the site's perimeter and from the slopes of the dry ravines within the site. In this second collection Inca as well as several pre-Inca pottery shards, possibly dating to the Huari Period (Middle Horizon), were recovered.

Plate 10. A view of Puma Orco from Maukallaqta

Plate 11. Puma Orco

Excavations were conducted in zone 1 of the site during 1986 (Fig. 17).[5] One of the most important results of these excavations was the discovery of pre-Inca remains beneath building 1 of the second terrace section (Figs. 17 and 18). These remains included two parallel, curving walls and a number of ceramic fragments (Fig. 19). The bright colors used on several of the painted ceramic finds and the presence of steep, straight-sided bowls with vertical band motifs suggest a Huari influence. As such, these remains have been tentatively dated to the Huari Period (Middle Horizon) of the Cuzco region; however, additional collections and radiocarbon dates are needed to confirm this classification.

Other important excavations at Maukallaqta were conducted in the inner chamber and the outer chamber of zone 1 (Fig. 17). The inner chamber of Maukallaqta is the most intriguing section of the ruins. Its central location off the central court, its unique niche entrance, and its independence from the rest of the site mark the inner chamber as an area of special activities. Four rooms of the inner chamber (numbers 1, 3, 4, and 5 in Fig. 17) were selected for excavation in the hope that the artifacts recovered would yield information concerning the nature of this unusual enclosure (Bauer 1990a, 1992). During the course of excavation, however, it was discovered that earlier cleaning operations at the site had destroyed most of the Inca floors. Excavations beneath the Inca structures of the inner chamber did, however, yield several pottery fragments, similar to the "Huari-related" finds discovered beneath building 1 of the second terrace section.

Additional excavations were also conducted in room 2 of the outer chamber. Near the center of the room a looted burial was found. The burial contained the remains of one adult skeleton, twenty-three ceramic items, two marine shells, a gold llama, two fragments of metal sheet (one gold and one silver), a silver *tumi* (knife), two silver *tupus* (pins), and various scraps of silver. All of the ceramic and metal items found in the burial date to the Inca Period (Bauer 1990a, 1992).

The Role of State Facilities in the Province of Paruro

The site of Maukallaqta is exceptional for the Province of Paruro. The relatively large size of the site and the presence of fine Inca stonework indicate that this ruin was of considerable importance to the Province of Paruro as well as to the Inca state. The most obvious functional explanation for the site would be that Maukallaqta was a center for Inca administration over ethnic groups that lived south of the imperial capital.

Recent comparative work in other Inca administration centers in the Andes, including Huánuco Pampa (Morris and Thompson 1985), Hatun Xauxa (D'Altroy 1981), and Pumpu (LeVine 1985), does not,

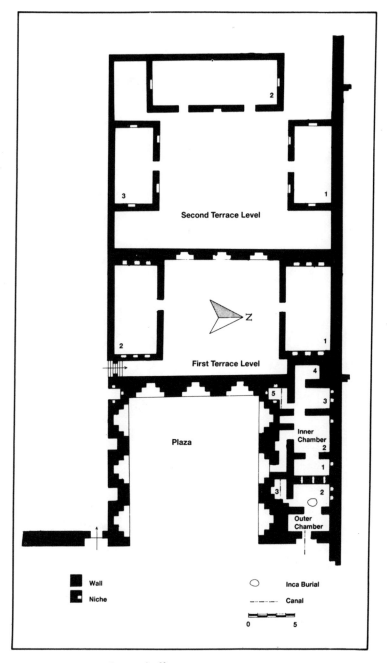

Figure 17. Zone 1 of Maukallaqta

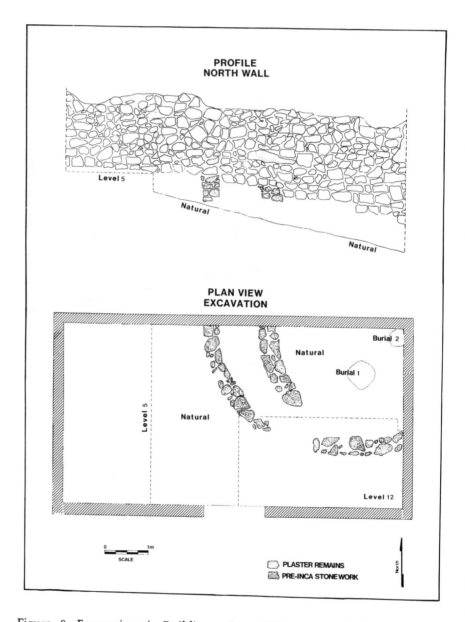

Figure 18. Excavations in Building 1, Second Terrace Level of Zone 1

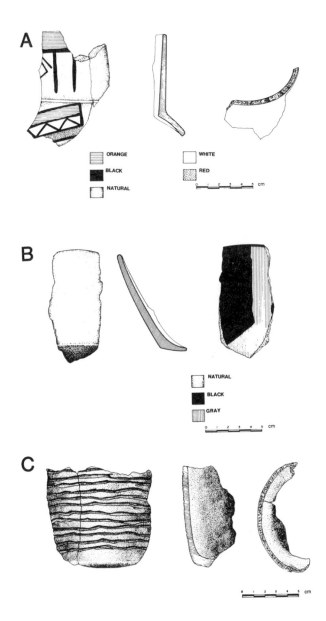

Figure 19. Ceramics from Excavations in Building 1, Second Terrace Level of Zone 1: *A*, Huari Period; *B*, Huari Period; *C*, Unknown

however, support this suggestion. For example, after an in-depth study of the major Inca state facilities in the north-central highlands of Peru, LeVine (1985:480) concludes that meeting the demands of state communication and transportation was the "guiding principle" in the selection of site locations for Inca administrative centers. The construction of Maukallaqta, well off the major southern Inca road and on a relatively high mountain shelf in a small tributary valley, would not be consistent with this principle.

Recent studies have also indicated that Inca administrative centers played a critical role in the collection, storage, and redistribution of state goods.[6] This role is most apparent in the number of storage houses that surround various regional centers. Maukallaqta provides a clear contrast to these sites and their emphasis on storage facilities. There are no buildings in Maukallaqta comparable to the square and circular storage structures adjacent to the administrative centers of Huánuco Pampa, Hatun Xauxa, and Pumpu.[7] Given Maukallaqta's construction on a mountain shelf off the major thoroughfare of the region and the lack of storage structures at the site, it is difficult to demonstrate that Maukallaqta functioned as a regional administrative center responsible for the collection, storage, and redistribution of surplus goods produced by the surrounding ethnic groups.

A number of independent archaeological and historical studies conducted in the 1940s by Muelle (1945) and Pardo (1946) and in the late 1980s by Urton (1989, 1990) and myself (Bauer 1988, 1991) have suggested that the ruins of Maukallaqta may have been explicitly associated with the Pacariqtambo origin myth of the Inca, and that its function may have been ritually based rather than concerned with the production and storage of local goods. This myth, recorded in over twenty separate chronicles, recalls the emergence of the first Inca, Manco Capac, from a cave called Tambotoco at a place called Pacariqtambo (Sarmiento de Gamboa [1572, Bks. 11, 12] 1906:33–37; Polo de Ondegardo [1571] 1916:49–50; Cobo [1653] 1956:64; Cabello Balboa [1586] 1951:260; Murúa [1615] 1962:21). The myth describes Manco Capac's northward journey from Pacariqtambo to the Cuzco Valley and his battle with the local inhabitants and the establishment of a new dynastic order in Cuzco. The members of the ruling elite of Cuzco at the time of the Spanish Conquest were thought to be the direct descendants of Manco Capac and were viewed as the legitimate rulers of the Inca state. The association between Manco Capac and the Inca nobility is most eloquently stated by Juan de Santa Cruz Pachacuti Yamqui Salcamayhua ([1613] 1950:273) as he describes the elite of Cuzco as the *mancopchurincuzco* (Cuzco Sons of Manco [Capac]).

There is sufficient historical and architectural information to suggest that the ruins of Maukallaqta represented a religious center for the Inca and were directly linked to the Pacariqtambo origin myth (Muelle 1945; Pardo 1946, 1957; Bauer 1988, 1991; Urton 1989, 1990). For example, Cobo, after discussing a version of the Pacariqtambo origin myth, writes:

> . . . demás de lo que contienen las dichas fábulas, tengo por no pe-queño indicio en apoyo de mi opinión el haber los Incas fundado un pueblo en aquel asiento de Pacarictampu y labrado en él, para ilus-trarle, un grandioso y real palacio con un templo suntuosísimo que aún duran hoy día sus ruinas y se ven en ellas algunos ídolos y esta-tuas de piedra . . . (Cobo [1653, Bk. 2, Chap. 3] 1956:64)

> Moreover, besides what is contained in the aforementioned fa-bles, I consider it to be no small indication in favor of my view that the Inca had founded a town on the site of Pacariqtambo, and that they built on it, in order to make it famous, a magnificent royal pal-ace with a splendid temple. The ruins of this palace and temple re-main even today, and in them some stone idols and statues are seen. (Cobo 1979:107)

This passage from Cobo is important because it appears to describe an Inca ruin south of Cuzco that was dedicated to the mythical progeni-tor of the Inca. It is almost certain that Cobo's account of a "magnifi-cent royal palace" built by the Inca as a monument to Manco Capac refers to the site of Maukallaqta. More specifically, his description of a "splendid temple" may refer to the central court and chamber area of the site. The "stone idols and statues" he mentions may have been the two pumas carved on the summit of Puma Orco.[8]

A second important document that links the ruins of Maukallaqta with the site of Pacariqtambo has been found by Urton in the Archivo del Ministerio de Agricultura: Cuzco (AMAC) (Urton 1989, 1990). The document is a petition from ayllu Pachecti, located on a small hill im-mediately south of Puma Orco and Maukallaqta, to the Ministerio de Trabajo y Asuntos Indígenas requesting official recognition of Pa-checti as a rural community. In the petition, the author, Hilario Ga-lindo, uses archival documents dating back to 1614 to record the mod-ern land boundaries of the community. Galindo specifically states that the "old town of Pacariqtambo" lies within the lands owned by ayllu Pachecti (Urton 1989, 1990; AMAC, Expediente #4281, 1964:34v). Since the ruins of Maukallaqta represent the only large set of ruins within the boundaries of ayllu Pachecti, there can be little doubt that the reference to "the old town of Pacariqtambo" in the document refers to Maukallaqta. The change of the site's name from Pacariqtambo to Maukallaqta most likely resulted from the Spanish reducción movement. During this movement the scattered ayllu settlements, which formed the moiety system of the Pacariqtambo region, were reduced to a central location. With the establishment of the reducción settlement of San Pedro de Pacariqtambo in 1571, the former Inca installation would have been referred to as the old town of Pacariqtambo or simply Maukallaqta (*Mauka* = old, *llaqta* = city).

The probable association of the Pacariqtambo origin myth with the ruins of Maukallaqta provides information that is useful in interpreting the function of certain sectors of the site. The central court of Maukallaqta with its fine Inca stonework, large triple-jamb niches, and adjacent chambers can be interpreted as the ceremonial center of the site. Given the likely affiliation of Maukallaqta with the Pacariqtambo origin myth of the Inca, it may be suggested that this unusual architectural feature may have been used as an oracle complex or temple for Manco Capac. If the inner chamber did house an image of the first mythical Inca, then the unusual niche-entrance between the central court and the inner chamber may have represented a window (or cave) through which an image of Manco Capac might have emerged on certain ceremonial occasions. In addition, the outcrop of Puma Orco may represent the very cave from which the Inca believed their ancestors first appeared on the earth. If this is the case, these Inca state installations were not specifically concerned with state administration over the region south of Cuzco, but instead are monuments constructed by the ruling elite of Cuzco to commemorate their mythical progenitor.

Summary and Discussion

Twenty aerial kilometers due south of Cuzco in the District of Pacariqtambo lie two important archaeological ruins: Maukallaqta and Puma Orco. As these two sites represented the largest and best-known Inca sites in the Province of Paruro, they have been specifically described in this chapter. Surface collections and excavations at Maukallaqta have yielded Inca pottery, as well as a number of pre-Inca shards that most likely date to the Huari Period (Middle Horizon). The standing stone structures, especially those near the central court area of the site, conform to the canons of Inca architecture, suggesting that the central zones of the site were constructed, or extensively rebuilt, after the consolidation of the Inca state. A comparison of Maukallaqta with regional centers of Inca administration elsewhere in the empire emphasizes the unusual location and architectural features of this Inca installation. In addition, the lack of storage structures at the site of Maukallaqta further weakens the suggestion that Maukallaqta was used as a regional center for Inca administration.

In the above discussion it has been suggested that the site of Mauka-llaqta, rather than being built as an Inca administration center for the southern Cuzco hinterland, was built as a temple complex related to the origin myth of Manco Capac. The recovery of pre-Inca remains, possibly dating to the Huari Period, under Maukallaqta indicates that this mountain shelf was inhabited long before the development of the Inca state. These earlier remains suggest that the Inca may have incorporated a pre-Inca site into the Pacariqtambo origin myth. The absence of Killke Period remains at Maukallaqta—indicated by the results of our limited surface collections and test excavations—is also intriguing. As discussed in earlier chapters, numerous archaeological sites in the Province of Paruro were occupied during both the Killke and Inca periods. It has also been suggested, based on the similar Killke and Inca period subsistence-settlement patterns of the survey region, that the development of the Inca state brought few changes to the economic organizations south of Cuzco. The construction of Maukallaqta by the Inca may be an important exception to the continuity of settlements in the region through the Killke and Inca periods. If the site's unusual qualities are related to its probable function as a palace and temple complex built in honor of Manco Capac, then the ruins may stand as a retrospective glorification by the Inca of a mythohistorical past that occurred during or just before the period of imperial expansionism.

8.

The Ayllu and Moiety Organizations of the Tambo Ethnic Group during the Killke and Inca Periods

THE KILLKE AND INCA PERIOD subsistence-settlement systems of the Province of Paruro were examined in Chapter 6. The purpose of this chapter is to investigate the social organizations south of Cuzco during the same periods. The Inca Period moiety structure of the Pacariqtambo region is investigated in the first section, to better understand the social organizations of the Inca de Privilegio groups surrounding Cuzco.[1] This examination then serves as an archaeologically and historically grounded base line through which the investigation is extended back into the Killke Period. In this way the chapter, designed primarily as a case study, provides a means to examine the moiety structure of the area during the period of early Inca state formation and a chance to discuss how the social organizations of the Cuzco ethnic groups were affected by the processes of state growth.

Principles of Andean Dual Organization

Indigenous expressions of dual social organization are found in various South American societies. These societies range in their level of cultural complexity from the hunting and gathering tribes of the Amazon forest to the complex polities of the north coast of Peru and the empire of the Inca. The pre-Hispanic, pan-American presence of moieties, indigenously defined by binary contrasts with internal, hierarchical ranking (higher:lower, male:female, right:left), and their continued use in many traditional regions today lend credence to the antiquity and the stability of this structuring principle (Turner 1984).[2]

Like other moiety systems, Andean moieties are expressed in terms of ranked pairs that, in the Quechua-speaking sectors of the Andes, are most frequently called *hanansaya* (upper division) and *hurinsaya* (lower division). Essential in this structuring principle are the hierarchical character of the two sets and the perspective that two apparently opposing values together form a unity (Turner 1984:338). For example, Bernabé Cobo writes:

> Hicieron en todo su reino estos Incas la misma división en que estaba repartida la ciudad del Cuzco, de *Hanan Cuzco* y *Hurin Cuzco*; dividiendo cada pueblo y cacicazgo en dos partes o bandos dichos *hanansaya* y *hurinsaya*, que suena el barrio alto y el barrio bajo, o la parte y bando superior y el bando inferior; y puesto caso que los nombres denotan desigualdad entre estos dos bandos, con todo eso, no lo la había más que en esta preeminencia y ventaja, que era ser preferido en asiento y lugar el bando de *hanansaya* a el de *hurinsaya*; al modo que en cortes unas ciudades preseden a otras en lugar y en hablar primero. En todo lo demás eran iguales, y por tan buenos eran tenidos los *hurinsayas* como los *hanansayas*. (Cobo [1653, Bk. 2, Chap. 24] 1956:112)

The Incas made the same division throughout all of their kingdom that they had made in dividing Cuzco into Hanan Cuzco and Hurin Cuzco. Thus they divided each town and *cacicazgo* (dominion of a native chief) into two parts, known as the upper district and the lower district, or the superior part or faction and the inferior; and even though these names denote inequality between these two groups, nevertheless, there was none, except for this pre-eminence and advantage, which was that the groups of *hanansaya* got preference in seating and place over those of *hurinsaya*; this is the same thing done at court, where some cities precede others in place and in speaking first. In everything else they were equal, and the *hurinsaya* people were considered to be as good as the *hanansaya* people. (Cobo 1979:195)

Andean populations have, however, also developed a unique social structure in which moiety relationships are expressed in hierarchical terms of social prestige (ruler:ruled, Inca:non-Inca, conquering outsider:dominated local peoples). A fine description of the symbolic divisions that separated Andean moieties is provided by Luis Capoche:

> Y los hanansayas, que quiere decir la parcialidad de arriba, tenían el primer grado de nobleza y acudían como gente militar a los llamamientos que hacía el Inca para la guerra; y los urinsayas, por quien se entiende la gente de abajo y el estado de la gente común [y] llana,

y los que servían de llevar las vituallas y mantenimientos de la gente de guerra. (Capoche [1585:55] 1959:140)

And the *hanansaya*, which means the group from above, held the first rank of nobility and they rallied as military people to the calls for war made by the Inca; and the *hurinsaya* are understood to be the people from below and the class of the common and simple people, who carried the provisions and necessities of the warriors.

This description emphasizes that while the contextual frame of the hanansaya and hurinsaya moiety division serves as an expression of equality in which two opposing values form a unity, the moiety division also reflects an asymmetrical prestige ranking linked to external powers. The *Hanan* (upper) moiety is thought to symbolically dominate the *Hurin* (lower) moiety, as the higher is generally associated with the outside state and the lower with the indigenous population of the region (Turner 1984; Zuidema 1964).

The Social Organization of Rural Andean Communities

Ethnographers and ethnohistorians have suggested that most rural Andean communities are, and were, conceptually divided into two contrasting halves, most frequently called hanansaya and hurinsaya. These moieties ideally contained an equal number of ayllus. Traditionally, the ayllus within each of the moieties carried a certain rank, based on their population and their historical social position. Although they were economically independent, the ayllus of each moiety, and at times the moieties themselves, would temporarily join together in communal work projects and religious festivals. During these moments the leading person of the most prestigious ayllu in each moiety would represent and organize that moiety's contributions.

The two separate sides of the rural moiety would be represented by two authorities, or *curacas* (leaders). The curaca of the hanansaya was frequently referred to by the Spanish as the *cacique principal* (principal chief), while the curaca of the hurinsaya was commonly called the *segunda persona* (second person). The social order of the moiety was reproduced at formal meetings with all of the ayllu leaders lining up, according to the rank of their respective ayllus, behind the curacas. When they were approached by higher-level authorities, the two moiety leaders would represent their respective moieties; in some cases the leader of the upper moiety would represent the community as a whole. Juan de Matienzo provides one of the clearest descriptions by a Spanish chronicler of the relationship that existed between the two moiety leaders and their subordinate authorities:

> En cada repartimiento o provincia hay dos parcialidades: una que se dice de *hanansaya*, y otra de *hurinsaya*. Cada parcialidad tiene un cacique principal que manda a los prencipales e indios de su parcialidad, y no se entremete a mandar a los de la otra, excepto que el curaca de la parcialidad de *hanansaya* es el principal de toda la provincia, y a quien el otro curaca de *hurinsaya* obedece en las cosas que dice él. Tiene el de *hanansaya* el mexor lugar de los asientos y en todo lo demás, que en esto guardan su orden. Los de la parcialidad de *hanansaya* se asientan a la mano derecha y los de *hurinsaya* a la mano izquierda, en sus asientos baxos que llaman *duos*, cada uno por su orden: los de *hurinsaya* a la izquierda tras su cacique principal, y los de *hanansaya* a la mano derecha, tras su curaca.
>
> Este de *hanansaya* es el principal de todos y tiene éste señorío sobre los de *hurinsaya*. Llama y hace juntas y gobierna en general, aunque no manda en particular. (Matienzo [1567, Pt. 1, Chap. 6] 1910:20–21)

> In each *repartimiento* or province there are two divisions: one is called *hanansaya*, and the other *hurinsaya*. Each division has a principal cacique who leads the principals and Indians of his division, and he does not interfere with those of the other division, except that the curaca of the hanansaya division is the principal lord of all the province; the other curaca of hurinsaya obeys him when he speaks. He of the hanansaya has the best position of the seats and in all the other places they repeat this order. Those of the hanansaya division seat themselves at the right-hand side, and those from the hurinsaya at the left-hand side, in their low seats which they call *duos* each one in order, those of hurinsaya at the left behind their principal cacique and those from hanansaya at the right hand, behind their curaca.
>
> This leader from hanansaya is the principal of all and he has domination over those of hurinsaya. He calls and makes assemblies and governs in general, although he does not rule in particular.

In summary, the unique model of Andean social organization presented by ethnohistorians and ethnographers for the Inca and later-period communities is one of economically independent ayllus ranked according to size and inherent social position. Ayllus were organized into village moieties. The symmetrical relationships of the moieties were essential to the reproduction of the community as a whole, but

they also expressed a hierarchical order in terms of their relative relations with the outside state. This structuring principle is thought to
have been present at all levels of Inca social organization including
Cuzco and the empire (Guamán Poma de Ayala [1615] 1980:337), the regional suyus of the empire (Capoche [1585] 1959:140; Julien 1983;
Bouysse-Cassagne 1986), incorporated kingdoms (Capoche [1585]
1959:140; Diez de San Miguel [1567] 1964:64–70; Murra 1968), and lesser
polities (Matienzo [1567] 1910:20–21). Or, more concisely stated, it is
thought that the local, or community, system of dual organization
during Inca times was reproduced at all levels of the society and that
the form of the empire as a whole was a reproduction of the basic
dualistically organized community.

The Inca Period Moiety Structure of the Pacariqtambo Region: Historical Evidence

At the time of Viceroy Toledo's 1571 reducción movement, the Inca system of four large regional suyus was still being used by the Spaniards to
administer the Cuzco territory.[3] Although records concerning the reducción movement in Chinchaysuyu, Antisuyu, and Collasuyu have yet to
be located, a document in the Archivo General de Indias (Sevilla) presents
a condensed description of the reducciones created in Cuntisuyu (Ulloa
1909). This document, entitled Visita general de los yndios del Cuzco,
año de 1571, provincia Condesuyo (General Inspection of the Indians of
Cuzco, of the Year 1571, Province of Cuntisuyu), gives a brief description
of the pueblos nuevos (new towns) created by the Spaniards and names
the smaller indigenous settlements, referred to as pueblos viejos (old
towns), which were consolidated in the new towns.[4] According to this
document, a town called San Pedro de Quiñoca, also known in the same
document as San Pedro de Pacariqtambo, was created by "reducing" ten
or eleven smaller settlements.[5]

> Pueblo nombrado san pedro de quinoca juntáronse honce pueblos
> que son pachete carnacollo quinoaca achacari marcagalla guancho y
> anchacalla cuno aupa, guatupasta naivapuca en que ubo 248 yndios
> tributarios todos de don luis palomino están 4 leguas del cuzco . . .
> (Ulloa 1909:334)

> The town called San Pedro de Quiñoca united eleven towns, which
> are Pachecti, Qarhuacalla, Quinhuara, Aqchakar, Marcagalla, Guay-
> cho and Yanchacalla, Cuno, Ccoipa, Guatupasta, and Nayhuapuca,
> in which were 248 tribute-paying Indians, all of Don Luis Palomino;
> they are 4 leagues from Cuzco . . .

Additional information concerning the indigenous, pre-reducción settlements of the Pacariqtambo area is presented in other sixteenth- and seventeenth-century administrative documents (Urton 1984, 1988, 1989, 1990). These sources suggest that the eleven pueblos viejos listed as reduced into the town of Pacariqtambo in 1571 represented individual ayllu settlements.[6] They also suggest that a moiety system integrated the settlements of the Pacariqtambo region on the eve of the Spanish reducción movement.

The earliest document containing information on the social organization of the Pacariqtambo region, which was found by Luis Miguel Glave in the Archivo General de la Nación (Lima), dates to 1568, three years before Viceroy Toledo's reducción movement was begun.[7] The document records a petition placed by the representatives of various pueblos in the repartimiento of Pacariqtambo to appoint Don Pedro Calla Piña as the cacique principal of the repartimiento. The document specifically describes those attending the meeting as leaders of separate settlements (pueblos), rather than as leaders of separate ayllus, as they were called after the creation of the reducción. Present at the meeting were the principal leaders of six settlements, including Pachecti, Qarhuacalla, Quinhuara, Aqchakar, Cuño, and Ccoipa. The names of these six towns not only correspond with six of the towns mentioned in the 1571 document, but are listed in the same relative order:

> Don Francisco Paucar, principal del Pueblo de *Pachicti* y Sebastian Curillo, principal del pueblo de *Caruacalla* y Bautista Princoncho del pueblo de *Quinuara* y don Luis Sutic, principal del pueblo de Acchacara [?] y don Diego Calla Paucar, principal del pueblo de *Cuño* y don Diego Chalco, principal del pueblo de *Cuypa*, que todas se incluyen en el repartimiento de Pacaritambo de la encomienda de don Luis Palomino, sujetos a don Pedro Calla Piña su cacique y senor principal. Dan poder a Garcia de Esquivel en la Real Audiencia de Charcas y a don Luis Paucar, Francisco Rauraua, Bernabe Chalco, Andrés Yaure y don Alonso Chalco, que estan ausentes, a todos juntos para que representandolos pidan a Su Magestad y a su Real Audiencia de Charcas que nombren al dicho Pedro Calla Piña por su cacique principal y señor de todo el repartimiento de Pacaritambo . . . (Urton 1990:146, no. 3)

> Don Francisco Paucar, principal of the town of Pachecti and Sebastian Curillo, principal of the town of Qarhuacalla, and Bautista Princoncho of the town of Quinhuara, and Don Luis Sutic, principal of the town of Aqchakar, and Don Diego Calla Paucar, principal of the town of Cuño, and Don Diego Chalco, principal of the town

of Ccoipa, which all include the repartimiento of Pacariqtambo of the *encomienda* (land and inhabitants granted to a Spaniard) of Don Luis Palomino, subjects of Don Pedro Calla Piña their cacique and principal lord. They give power to García de Esquival in the Royal Audience of Charcas and to Don Luis Paucar, Francisco Rauraua, Bernabé Chalco, Andrés Yaure, and Don Alonso Chalco, who are absent, together representing them, they ask his Majesty and his Royal Audience of Charcas to nominate the mentioned Pedro Calla Piña as their main principal cacique and Lord of all the repartimiento of Pacariqtambo . . .

Besides listing the leaders of six separate towns by name, this document also lists the names of five additional men who were absent from the meeting, but who joined in the request. It is probable that these five men represent the leaders of the five additional ayllus of the Pacariqtambo repartimiento listed in the later 1571 reducción document.[8]

A third document yielding evidence on the sixteenth-century social organization of the Pacariqtambo region has been found by Urton in a private collection in Cuzco. The document is dated 1594, some twenty-three years after the reducción movement, and contains a brief list of ayllu land holdings surrounding the reducción of Pacariqtambo. This 1594 document yields a list of ayllu names that is very similar to those found in the earlier 1568 pre-reducción document and the 1571 reducción document. The ayllus recorded for the Pacariqtambo region in 1594 include Nayhua, Quinhuara, Aqchakar, Qarhuacalla, Pachecti, San Miguel, Pirca, Ccoipa, Guaycho, and Marcagalla. Several other later documents for the Pacariqtambo region, primarily censuses from the Province of Paruro, show a remarkable continuation of ayllu names into the nineteenth and twentieth centuries (Urton 1984, 1988, 1989, 1990). These later documents list the ayllu of Pacariqtambo in relation to the hanansaya and hurinsaya moiety divisions of the region (Table 5).

Additional ethnographic data were recorded by Urton during his work in the modern reducción of Pacariqtambo. Urton (1984) found that the majority of the ayllus listed in the sixteenth-century documents correspond with the ayllus of the modern community. Urton has also identified various fields, ridges, and hilltops that are associated by his local informants with the ancestral locations of the modern Pacariqtambo ayllus. A summary of the ethnographic and historical ayllu and moiety information for the Pacariqtambo region is presented in columns 3–6 of Table 5.[9]

Besides identifying the names and possible locations of the original reducción ayllus of the Pacariqtambo region, the ethnographic and

Table 5. Ayllus of the Pacariqtambo Region ca. A.D. 1000–1595

	1	2	3	4	5	6
	Killke Period	Inca Period	Ayllu Origin Places[a]	1568[b]	1571[c]	1595[d]
Hanansaya						
1	?	?	Coralpata		Naivapuca	Nayba
2	Killke	Inca	Quinhuara	Quinuara	Quinoaca	Quimbara
3	Killke	Inca	Aqchakar	Acchacara	Achacari	Achacari
4	None	Inca	Qarhuacalla	Caruacalla	Carnacollo	Carbacalla
5	Killke	Inca	Pachecti	Pachicti	Pachete	Pachite
Hurinsaya						
A	None	None	Sullukllapata	Cuno	Cuno	San Miguel
B	Killke	Inca	Jurinka	—	—	Pirca
C	Killke	Inca	Ccoipa	Cuypa	Aupa	Coypa
D	Killke	Inca	Pukarapata	—	Guancho	Guaycho
E	Killke	Inca	Yanchacalla	—	Anchacalla Marcagalla Guatupasta	— Marcagalla

[a] Ethnographic research by Urton (1984).
[b] Urton (1989:188, 1990:72).
[c] Ulloa (1909).
[d] AMAC, Expediente #5877, 1944; Urton (1984, 1988, 1989, 1990).

historical sources have also aided in the identification of the boundary line that separated the hanansaya and hurinsaya moieties of the Pacariqtambo area during the sixteenth century. The territorial divisions between Andean moieties are frequently demarcated by natural boundaries, such as rivers and valleys, or by man-made divisions such as roads, footpaths, or irrigation systems (Anders 1986:718–719). In the region of Pacariqtambo, a major trail served as the territorial division between the hanansaya and hurinsaya moieties. The trail entered the Pacariqtambo region from the southwest, crossing the Apurimac River near the settlement of Nayhua. From Nayhua it first ran east, climbing the valley slope, and then turned northeast, eventually leading to Yaurisque. In the reducción of Pacariqtambo, the trail is called the *Chaupi Ñan* (Middle Way), and it still forms the territorial dividing line between the hanansaya and hurinsaya divisions of the community (Urton 1984, 1988, 1989, 1990).

The Inca Period Moiety Structure of the Pacariqtambo Region: Archaeological Evidence

The unusual combination of detailed ethnographic, historical, and archaeological data collected in the Pacariqtambo region provides an unprecedented opportunity to examine the ayllu and moiety organization of the region during Inca rule (Bauer 1987). As discussed in Chapter 6, systematic archaeological surveys conducted south of Cuzco in the Pacariqtambo region have identified a number of Inca Period sites. These sites vary greatly in size; the smallest appear to represent isolated homesteads and/or seasonal occupations, while the larger were most likely permanent villages. With the exception of the site of Maukallaqta and the carved rock outcrop of Puma Orco, the sites of the Pacariqtambo region are, in all likelihood, associated with the Tambo ethnic group, which occupied the region during the Inca Period (Sarmiento de Gamboa [1572] 1906:33; Garcilaso de la Vega [1609] 1945:41–42).

A synthesis of archaeological information gathered during the survey of the Pacariqtambo area and information collected from historical and ethnographic sources concerning the pre-reducción ayllu and moiety structure of the Pacariqtambo region is presented on Map 7. The locations of the thirteen largest Inca Period sites are marked with squares. The ten locations traditionally associated with ayllu settlements before the reducción, as described by Urton (1984), are marked with circles. These ayllu locations were further subdivided into two sets. The five locations that are associated with the origin points for the hanansaya ayllus are featured with solid circles, while the five as-

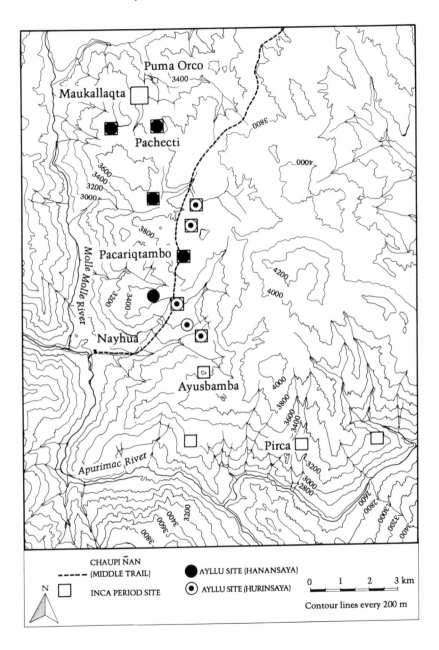

Map 7. The Inca Period Ayllus and Moieties of Pacariqtambo

sociated with the hurinsaya ayllus are distinguished with a circle and a central dot. The Chaupi Ñan is indicated with a dotted line.

Eight of the ten locations associated with the pre-reducción ayllus correspond with the locations of large Inca Period sites. The correlation of traditional toponyms with the names of ayllus listed in the sixteenth-century documents for the region, and with archaeological sites dating to the Inca Period, suggests that these remains do indeed mark the locations of the ayllus before the reducción movement (Table 5, Map 7). This being the case, these eight sites can be subdivided, according to their location in respect to the Chaupi Ñan, into two groups representing the Inca Period hanansaya and hurinsaya moiety divisions of the region (sites labeled 2, 3, 4, 5 and B, C, D, E, respectively, on Table 5 and Map 7).

The results of this ethnographic, historical, and archaeological synthesis are not, however, without ambiguities. One location, Coralpata (1 on Table 5 and Map 7), identified by local informants to be the location of ayllu Nayhua before the reducción movement, yielded minimal evidence of the Inca Period activities. The size of the Inca pottery scatter over Coralpata is substantially less than that found at the other ayllu locations and is more suggestive of a small or short-term occupation than of a permanent ayllu settlement. Nevertheless, the 1571 reducción document suggests that a settlement called Naivapuca (Nayhua Flower) was resettled into the reducción of Pacariqtambo. It is possible, however, that the pre-reducción location of ayllu Nayhua is situated beneath the present-day village of Nayhua, obscured by modern village construction activities and erosion. The location of the pre-reducción ayllu settlement of Nayhua beneath a place that bears its name would be consistent with the location and site names of several of the other ayllus in the Pacariqtambo region, including Quinhuara (2), Aqchakar (3), Qarhuacalla (4), Pachecti (5), Ccoipa (C), and Yanchacalla (E).

There are also two closely spaced fields called Sullukllapata and Santa Maria (A on Map 7), which, according to local informants, mark the traditional location of ayllu San Miguel (Urton 1984). No archaeological remains, however, were noted in these fields during our survey of the region. As the only ayllu of the Pacariqtambo moiety system with a Spanish name, ayllu San Miguel is an anomaly in itself. It is first mentioned in the 1594 document and has, for at least the past century, held the prestigious position of first ayllu in hurinsaya. During prehistoric times the ayllu may have been known as Cuño, an apparently high-ranking ayllu of the lower moiety.[10] The exact location of ayllu Cuño before the 1571 reducción is currently unknown.[11]

Further ambiguities exist in the presence of several Inca sites not described in the reducción documents or identified by Urton during his ethnographic work in the region as traditional ayllu locations. These include locations I, II, III, IV, and V on Map 7.[12] Four of the Inca sites, locations II, III, IV, and V, contain archaeological remains that are similar to those found at the eight locations associated with pre-reducción ayllus. It should be noted, however, that these four sites are located in isolated sections of the Apurimac River Valley, south of the densest area of Inca Period occupation. It appears from their remote locations that some or all of these sites may have been peripheral occupations of the Inca Period Pacariqtambo moiety system.[13] Additional archaeological and ethnographic investigations will be needed at these more remote sites to determine the nature of their articulation with the ayllus and the moiety system of the Pacariqtambo region during the Inca Period.

The largest Inca Period site in the Pacariqtambo area is Maukallaqta (I on Map 8). The large size and stone architecture of the site set it apart from the other Inca Period occupations of the region. Evidence has been presented suggesting that the site of Maukallaqta represents a state facility related to the Pacariqtambo origin myth of the Inca; as such, the site may have functioned independently of the local moiety system.

The Killke Period Moiety Structure of the Pacariqtambo Region

Archaeological research conducted in the region of Pacariqtambo indicates that the Inca Period population was concentrated in twelve settlements. Ethnographic and historical research suggests that at least eight of the twelve Inca Period settlements in the region represent individual ayllu occupations, and that these separate ayllu occupations were organized into two territorial moieties. Using this archaeologically and historically based model of the Inca Period moiety organization as a base line, the Killke Period social organization of the region will be examined in this section to determine the effect that the development of the Inca state had on the social organization of the Inca de Privilegio groups living south of Cuzco.

Regional survey data indicate that the Killke Period settlement pattern in the Pacariqtambo region is nearly identical to that of the Inca Period. This is illustrated on Map 8, where the locations of the major sites dating to the Killke Period in the Pacariqtambo region are represented by triangles. As can be seen, seven of the eight sites identified as Inca Period ayllu settlements were also occupied during the Killke Period (Table 5 and Map 8). These include the sites of Quinhuara (2), Aqchakar (3), Pachecti (5), Jurinka (B), Ccoipa (C), Pukarpata (Guaycho)

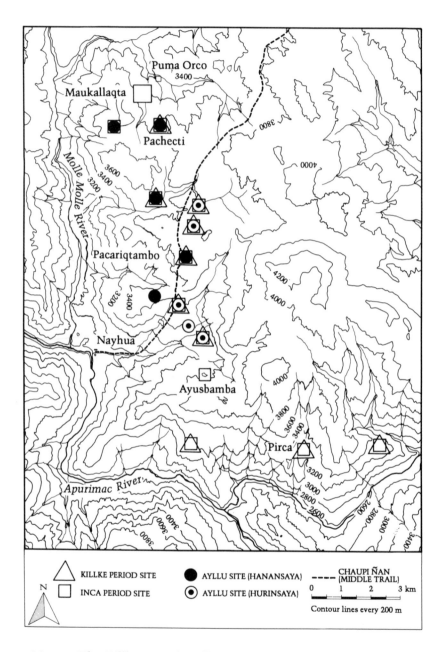

Map 8. The Killke Period Ayllus and Moieties of Pacariqtambo

(D), and Yanchacalla (E). In addition, three of the four large Inca Period sites for which we have no historical references, sites Ayapata (III), Pirca Moco (IV), and Huichuro (V) on Maps 7 and 8, also yielded evidence of Killke Period occupation. The presence of Killke and Inca period remains at these three sites indicates a long-term occupation and suggests that they indeed represent the locations of ayllu occupations rather than state installations. Two of the twelve large Inca Period settlements did not, however, provide surface evidence of a Killke Period occupation. These sites include the ayllu settlement of Qarhuacalla (4), located in the northwest corner of the moiety system, and the site of Ayusbamba (II), located in the southern area of the Pacariqtambo region. Additional surface collections and test excavations are needed at these sites to evaluate the nature of their Inca occupations.

In all, Table 5 and Maps 7 and 8 reveal a remarkable continuity of ayllu settlements in the Pacariqtambo region from the Killke to the Inca periods. This evidence suggests that the development of the Inca state brought few physical changes to the social organization of the Tambo and that the Inca Period moiety system of the region may have been a direct continuation of an earlier system, dating to at least the Killke Period.

Summary and Discussion

The moiety systems of present-day Andean communities have frequently been the subject of ethnographic research, and ethnohistorians have long speculated on the moiety-based structure of the Inca Empire. The reproduction of dual systems of social organization at all levels of social hierarchy in the Andes, from rural communities to imperial realms, suggests that moiety systems are core principles of Andean society, constituting key units of study in Andean state organization. The Pacariqtambo test case has shown that we are able to apply these principles of social organization to the settlement patterns of Killke and Inca period archaeological sites. The study highlights the fact that moiety and ayllu affiliations provide overarching models of Andean rural organization that should be included in regional interpretations of indigenous populations in the Andes. In addition, this study underscores the need to integrate ethnographic, historical, and archaeological data sets in the investigation of prehistoric moiety divisions. Until archaeological correlates for moiety systems are clearly identified, such an integrated approach not only is preferable, but is essential in the reconstruction of prehistoric social organizations.

The research findings described in this chapter suggest that eight Inca Period sites in the Pacariqtambo region represent, in all probability, the locations of specific ayllus of the Tambo ethnic group before the reducción of 1571. Ethnographic and historical data have enabled us to divide these eight sites into the two indigenously defined moieties of hanansaya and hurinsaya, and to identify the trail which formed the moiety division. The continuous occupation of the ayllu sites from the Killke to the Inca period indicates that the Inca moiety system, as identified through ethnographic research and recorded in the early colonial documents, may have been a direct continuation of a Killke Period system of dual organization. The Inca state authority is represented in the region by the site of Maukallaqta. This Inca facility is located both physically and conceptually on the margin of the Pacariqtambo moiety system. On the basis of this evidence, it is suggested that the process of state development had little effect on the regional social organization of Pacariqtambo and that the social organization of the Tambo continued relatively unchanged despite the emergence of the Cuzco region as a pan-Andean power.

The Pacariqtambo region has been used as a test case to illustrate the spatial organization of rural moiety systems during the Killke and Inca periods. Continuity of settlement occupation from the Killke to the Inca period in the Province of Paruro is not, however, limited to the Pacariqtambo region. As noted in Chapter 6, a remarkable continuity of Killke and Inca period sites was also observed in the regions of Yaurisque, Paruro, and Colcha. These regions are known to have been inhabited by members of the Chillque and Masca ethnic groups. Historical and ethnographic evidence, although currently incomplete, strongly suggests that these Inca de Privilegio groups were also organized along similar lines. The fact that a large ayllu in the modern community of Yaurisque is called hanansaya indicates that the Masca may also have been organized into moieties at the time of the 1571 reducción movement. Remnants of a moiety division also survive in the town of Paruro, where a major ayllu of the community also retains the name of hanansaya. South of the Apurimac River, the reducciones of Araypallpa and Colcha have retained their basic forms of dual organization, containing two and four ayllus, respectively (Poole 1984).[14] The small community of San Lorenzo, within the District of Colcha, is also composed of two moieties, each of which is divided into two ayllus. Further south is the community of Accha, which until recently was divided into Hanan and Hurin divisions by a small stream that crossed through its central plaza (Villanueva Urteaga 1982:471; Decoster 1989). These manifestations of dual social organization indicate that many of the regions in the Province of Paruro, and perhaps all of the ethnic groups under study here, were organized by separate moiety systems at the time of Inca rule. The archaeological evidence from the Pacariqtambo region suggests that moiety divisions in the region south of Cuzco were already established during the Killke Period and that they remained relatively unchanged until the arrival of the Spaniards and the implementation of the reducciones.

9.
Summary and Conclusion

MANY ANDEAN SCHOLARS, using information presented in the Spanish chronicles, have accepted what I have called the traditional, or event-based, account of Inca state formation. This theory suggests that before the Chanca war, Cuzco was a small village occupied by the Inca and that regional conflicts separated the various ethnic groups of the area. According to this model, external pressure exerted on the Cuzco region by the Chanca provided a unique situation in which the charismatic leader Pachacuti Inca Yupanqui could seize power from his father, Viracocha Inca, and unite the regional ethnic groups. It is suggested that during the unification process of the Cuzco region, the Inca, under the direction of Pachacuti Inca Yupanqui, reorganized the regional ethnic settlements and relocated the formerly fractious groups. The ethnic groups of the region formed alliances with the Inca, becoming Inca de Privilegio, and centralized power was established in Cuzco. After the unification and reorganization of the Cuzco region, Pachacuti Inca Yupanqui began to expand the Inca state beyond the confines of the Cuzco Valley. Thus, according to the traditional account of state formation, the chaos of regional conflict in the prestate period ended as a result of a single event (the Inca victory over the Chanca) and the Andean world was transformed through the heroic actions of one individual (Pachacuti Inca Yupanqui).

In Chapters 1 through 8, I argue against the use of the traditional explanation of state growth and the methodological individualism that supports it, in favor of a more processual approach. In doing so, I have presented archaeological data that appear to diverge from the information presented in the Spanish accounts and that throw literal interpretations of the chronicles into a questionable light. Furthermore, I have mobilized evidence that suggests that incipient state growth in the

Cuzco region was marked by the gradual consolidation and centralization of economic authority in Cuzco during the Killke Period rather
than through the heroic actions of a single leader. If this interpretation
is correct, we can no longer base our understanding of the Andean
past on literal readings of the chronicles. Archaeological research in
the Cuzco region on the development of the Inca state, consequently,
assumes great importance. Such research forms an independent means
for examining the development of various social, political, and economic institutions and may, in time, lead to an understanding of the
central mechanisms involved in the processes of state development.

It should be noted, however, that the aim of this study has not been
to support or deny the historical validity of the Chanca war or the
existence of an Inca ruler named Pachacuti Inca Yupanqui. Nor do I
question the proposition that specific individuals can, and do, play important roles in a culture's history (Sahlins 1983, 1985). What I do question, however, is the meaningfulness of current approaches to Inca
history that focus exclusively on the role of a specific individual in the
development of the state. Rather than reaffirming that state development occurred in the Cuzco region through the heroic actions of a single political leader after the Inca's unexpected victory over the
Chanca, it is suggested that the centralization of regional authority
and the development of a stratified social hierarchy in the Cuzco region were already occurring during the Killke Period. Furthermore, I
maintain that incipient state formation was not localized within the
city of Cuzco, but incorporated the entire Cuzco region. In so doing, I
stress the need for a broader form of historical consciousness of the
development of the Inca state, extending beyond the study of kings
and battles, and attempting instead to examine classes of individuals
and entire geographic regions (Ricoeur 1980:10, Fogelson 1989:138).

This work began with a discussion of the social hierarchy of the
Cuzco region at the time of the Spanish Conquest. Using data provided in the chronicles of Garcilaso de la Vega (1609), Guamán Poma
de Ayala (1615), and Pachacuti Yamqui Salcamayhua (1613), the names
and social status of the various ethnic groups that were awarded the
honorary title of Inca de Privilegio by the Inca were discussed. The period during which these Inca de Privilegio groups were incorporated
into the Inca state becomes all-important for the study of state development. Subservient to Cuzco and yet allied with it, the Inca de Privilegio represented a large, tribute-paying social stratum that supported
the ruling elite in Cuzco through direct produce, and by occupying
low-level bureaucratic positions in state institutions. The development of a regional social class of producers marks the beginning of social stratification in the region, which is a widely recognized correlate

of early state growth (Cohen 1978:33). The traditional model of Inca state formation implies that the relations between various ethnic groups of the Cuzco region were hostile until the time of the Chanca war. According to this view, regional unity was achieved through the conquest and subjugation of the regional ethnic groups by the Inca. In contrast, this work suggests that the Masca, Chillque, and Tambo, the Inca de Privilegio occupying the region south of Cuzco, were under the influence or control of Cuzco as early as the Killke Period, and that the unification of the Cuzco region occurred not through military conquests by the Inca, but through nonmilitary means of unification, which began before the Chanca war is said to have taken place. The exact nature and scope of Killke Period unification in the Cuzco region remains, however, to be examined through further archaeological and historical research.

An examination of the Inca social hierarchy as provided by Guamán Poma de Ayala (1615) and Garcilaso de la Vega (1609) also indicated that the social stratification of the Cuzco region was legitimatized through references to the actions of the mythical founder of Cuzco, Manco Capac. The ruling Inca and the Inca of Royal Blood were believed to be the direct descendants of this culture hero, while the Inca de Privilegio are thought to have been only loosely affiliated with him. Since the founding of Cuzco by Manco Capac is said to have taken place in a primordial setting involving supernatural powers, the social stratification of the Inca was seen as both divinely sanctified and unchangeable. The legitimacy of the social order and centralized authority in the Cuzco region by the Inca is of particular interest to this study, since the largest state facility in the Province of Paruro, Maukallaqta, may have been built as a monument to Manco Capac.

In the third chapter, the current chronology for the Inca, based on dates provided in the Spanish chronicle of Cabello Balboa (1586), was reexamined. This reexamination revealed several problematic issues and emphasized the need to establish a chronology for state development independent of the sixteenth- and seventeenth-century Spanish chroniclers. In response to this need, an updated two-period chronology for Inca state development in the Cuzco region has been offered. The period of early state formation, named the Killke Period, is marked by the appearance of Killke and Killke-related pottery styles in the archaeological record. On the basis of radiocarbon dates from archaeological contexts with Killke pottery, it has been proposed that the Killke Period (or Early Inca Period) began at an earlier date than previously reported. Until more information is available from excavations in the Cuzco region, the chronological limits for Killke pottery production are tentatively set at ca. A.D. 1000 to ca. A.D. 1400. The

Inca Period, which follows the Killke Period, refers to the time of late state development and expansion. This period is associated with the appearance of Inca pottery and, to a lesser extent, Inca architectural forms. The Inca Period is thought to have begun around A.D. 1400 and to have continued until the Spanish invasion. It has been noted, however, that additional research is needed to clarify the transition between Killke and Inca ceramics in the Cuzco region, and more radiocarbon dates from excavations are required to confirm these tentative dates.

After introducing the specific survey region and discussing the research methodology, regional interactions south of Cuzco, reflected in the distribution of Killke Period pottery, were examined in Chapter 5. The closely related pottery styles of Killke and Colcha were defined and their distribution patterns in the research region were discussed. Excavations at the site of Tejahuasi, in which the two ceramic styles were found in a single sealed context, suggested that Killke and Colcha pottery were contemporaneous. The density of sites in the research region that contained these two ceramic styles was then examined to determine their probable loci of production and distribution. The density of sites containing Killke pottery was found to decrease in direct relation to their distance from Cuzco, indicating that Killke pottery may have been produced by Inca who were north of the research region. The density of Colcha pottery was, on the other hand, found to decrease as a function of distance from the village of Araypallpa, south of the Apurimac River in Chillque territory, suggesting that Colcha pottery was produced in this village during the Killke Period.

The identification of two separate but contemporaneous centers of Killke Period pottery manufacture provided a means to examine the trade networks that connected the ethnic groups of the Province of Paruro and the Inca during the emergence of the Inca state. It was suggested, based on the related design elements and motifs of Killke and Colcha pottery, that close contacts were maintained between the two separate centers of ceramic production. The overlapping ceramic distribution patterns of Killke and Colcha pottery also suggest that large-scale exchange networks and contacts existed between the various ethnic groups during the Killke Period. These regional lines of exchange and communication stand in general contrast to the customary vision of an Early Inca Period dominated by chronic regional warfare.

It was also noted that while Killke and Colcha pottery are stylistically similar, the distribution patterns of these two Killke Period ceramic styles are very different. The distribution range of Killke pottery was found to be more than double that of Colcha pottery, encompassing the entire Colcha distribution area. The large distribution range of

Killke pottery may reflect the greater influence that the Inca held in the Cuzco region during the Killke Period. In addition, a correlation was noted between the distribution of Killke pottery and the territories absorbed into the Inca state as regions of Inca de Privilegio, indicating that the Cuzco-based trade networks established during the Killke Period may have helped to unite the Cuzco ethnic groups as members of a single developing state. These observations suggest that the centralization of regional power had begun to coalesce in the Cuzco area and that, contrary to the traditional theory of Inca state development, the Cuzco Valley may have already emerged as the regional center for trade and exchange during the Killke Period.

A detailed examination of the subsistence-settlement systems of the Province of Paruro supports the conclusions drawn from the ceramic distribution patterns, further challenging the presuppositions of the event-based model of Inca state development. Archaeologists and ethnohistorians have suggested that before the Chanca war the Cuzco region was inhabited by a number of warring ethnic groups and that these groups were moved to new locations to suit the desires of Pachacuti Inca Yupanqui. Research in the Province of Paruro suggests that the Inca Period inhabitants lived in small communities. Village self-sufficiency was achieved through the simultaneous exploitation of a number of different ecological zones. Archaeological data from the Province of Paruro also indicate that few changes occurred in the subsistence-settlement systems of the survey region between the Killke and Inca periods. Instead of finding a series of abandoned Killke Period sites and the widespread appearance of new Inca Period settlements in the region, which would have supported the putative restructuring of the local subsistence-settlement systems by the Inca, it was found that all village sites occupied during the Killke Period continued to be occupied throughout the Inca Period.

The survey data for the Province of Paruro also provided an opportunity to examine the widely held view that the Killke Period was a time of chronic regional warfare. The existence of defensive works dating to the Killke Period in the research region would have indicated that a high level of regional conflict existed before the development of the Inca state, as suggested in the chronicles. However, systematic surveys in the Province of Paruro recorded no obvious evidence of Killke Period defensive structures. The subsistence-settlement systems of the survey region were found to comprise small, widely scattered, unprotected villages or hamlets generally located adjacent to areas of agricultural land, rather than large, fortified, nucleated communities located on ridges, which would have been suggestive of regional antagonism. The absence of any clear indication of Killke Period warfare in the

Province of Paruro and the continuous occupation of all major Killke Period sites into the Inca Period appear to be inconsistent with information drawn from the Spanish chronicles.

Dwyer, in an early survey of the Cuzco area, reported a similar pattern of small, unfortified Killke Period sites within the Cuzco Valley. Believing that the unfortified Killke Period sites of the Cuzco Valley were exceptional to the region as a whole, Dwyer suggested that the Cuzco Valley represented a relatively peaceful area in a region otherwise ravaged by war (Dwyer 1971:146). However, surveys south of Cuzco indicate that the pattern of unfortified Killke Period sites in the Cuzco Valley and their continued occupation into the Inca Period is not as exceptional to the region as was once thought.

Based on this evidence, it may be said that there are currently no clear archaeological data supporting the chronicles' depiction of regional warfare occurring in the Cuzco Valley or immediately to the south, nor are there any subsistence-settlement data from the Cuzco Valley or the Province of Paruro suggesting that a massive restructuring of the economic organization of the Cuzco region took place during or at the end of the Killke Period. Instead, it appears that the Cuzco Valley and the region to the south may have been culturally united, if not fully integrated, into some form of early Cuzco-based polity, or protostate, during the Killke Period. It is important to note, however, that most of the data for this study have been collected in the Province of Paruro. Additional systematic regional surveys and excavations are needed in other areas of the Cuzco region to explore the relationship the Inca held with other groups of Inca de Privilegio during the period of state formation.

Physical evidence for changes in the regional social organization of the Cuzco ethnic groups as a result of state growth are also examined in this work. Survey work in the area of Pacariqtambo indicates that members of the Tambo ethnic group occupied a number of small village settlements. On the basis of ethnographic and historical information provided by Urton (1984, 1988, 1989, 1990), it may be concluded that each of these small village sites represented the location of an individual ayllu before the Spanish reducción movement of 1571. A synthesis of ethnographic, historical, and archaeological information suggests that at least eight of the small village sites of the Tambo can be separated into moieties, each containing at least four sites, by a pre-Hispanic trail that crossed the region of Pacariqtambo. All but one of these small village sites were also occupied during the Killke Period. The continuous occupation of the small village sites during the Killke and Inca periods suggests that the emergence of the Inca state brought few changes to the social organization of the Pacariqtambo area, and that the Inca moiety system of the region is a continuation of an older, Killke Period system. Although the Pacariqtambo region was selected for intensive investigation, the continuous occupation of village sites from the Killke to the Inca period has been noted throughout the research region. In addition, ethnographic and historical data indicate that most of the other reducción villages of the research region, including Yaurisque, Paruro, Colcha, Araypallpa, San Lorenzo, and Accha, still retain remnants of former moiety divisions. Thus it appears that the ayllus of the other ethnic groups in the Province of Paruro were also organized, like those of the Tambo, into a series of regional moiety systems, and that these moiety systems continued relatively unchanged throughout the Killke and Inca periods. Questions remain, however, concerning the internal structure of these fundamental units of Inca society, their means of articulation with the state, and, on a more methodological level, the actual feasibility of identifying Inca moiety systems in an archaeological setting without ethnographic or historical information.

Although the development of the Inca state did not cause major physical changes in the subsistence-settlement systems or regional social organizations south of Cuzco, as predicted by the traditional theory of state development, a number of Inca facilities, including the site of Maukallaqta, were constructed in the area after the development of the state. Maukallaqta appears, however, to have been only marginally concerned with the administrative needs of the Inca de Privilegio living south of the capital. Historical data and architectural remains suggest that this site can be linked to the mythical origin of Manco Capac. Indeed, from the evidence currently available, it appears that Maukallaqta is the site of Pacariqtambo—of the Pacariqtambo origin myth of the Inca—and was built to commemorate the mythical progenitor of the Inca. As such, the site of Maukallaqta would have been used in legitimatizing the sacred status of the Inca of Royal Blood within the Cuzco-based political, economic, and ritual hierarchy.

In the general absence of large-scale, systematic archaeological surveys in the Cuzco region, ethnohistorians and archaeologists have relied on the heroic narratives presented in the sixteenth- and seventeenth-century Spanish chronicles to develop theories of state formation in the Cuzco region. The current, dominant view, which follows literal readings of the chronicles, is that before the Cuzco region was unified under centralized Inca rule, the area was occupied by a number of small antagonistic ethnic groups. The rapid cultural transformation of the Cuzco region from numerous raiding rural societies to an organized and expanding state is said to have been inspired by Pachacuti Inca Yupanqui, a young warrior-king of the Inca, after his military defeat of the Chanca. The present study, however, differs from previous research in the Cuzco region in that it questions the usefulness of literal interpretations of the Spanish chronicles to reconstruct pre-Hispanic events in the Cuzco Valley; it provides instead a regional, archaeologically based perspective on the question of state development. Most importantly, by discussing the development of the Inca state in terms of transformations of social, economic, and political institutions as reflected in an entire region, the study redirects the focus of research from Pachacuti Inca Yupanqui as the primary agent of historical change and begins to formulate a new social history of the Inca.

Notes

1. Introduction

1. The Quechua terms, toponyms, and personal names contained in this work are written according to their Hispanicized spelling as found in the Spanish chronicles and on modern maps. The English and Spanish plural form *s* is used in this text rather than the Quechua form (*kuna* or *cuna*).

Exceptions are made in certain cases where I cite important works of modern authors. In these cases, I continue the spellings that they provide (e.g., Xauxa [D'Altroy 1981] and Maukallaqta [Urton 1984, 1988, 1989, 1990]).

2. The term "Cuzco region" refers to an area, approximately 60 aerial kilometers in radius from the city of Cuzco, which was inhabited by Inca and Inca de Privilegio (Chapter 2).

3. The chronology for the Cuzco region is examined in Chapter 3.

4. All translations in this work are my own, except where otherwise noted.

5. The Department of Ayacucho is located approximately 200 km west of Cuzco.

6. Sarmiento de Gamboa's *Segunda parte de la Historia general llamada Indica . . .* (1572) provides a detailed description of the Inca's victory over the Chanca. Other important sources that contain extended discussions of the Chanca conflict include Betanzos (1551), Cieza de León (1553), Garcilaso de la Vega (1609), Pachacuti Yamqui Salcamayhua (1613), and Cobo (1653).

7. The appointed heir is said to have been Viracocha Inca's older son, Inca Urcon.

8. In short, Pachacuti, true to his name (Transformer of the Earth), formed the world anew, re-creating and redefining both time and space in the Cuzco region.

9. On a more general level, however, such literal readings of the Spanish chronicles and the "reconstruction" of the pre-Hispanic Andean past by ex-

tracting "historical" information from the chronicles are based within what the Annales school of French historiography has called a "positivist historical" approach. Paul Ricoeur (1980:8; also cited in Fogelson 1989:135), in a critical review of positivist history, has identified five major characteristics of this approach: (1) a position of neutral objectivity to the information present in the texts, (2) a reduction of history to the collection and critique of documents, (3) the assumption that the documents (in this case the Spanish chronicles) contain historical facts that need only be extracted, (4) the belief that explanation consists of relating particular events within a chronology imposed by the documents, and finally, perhaps the most important characteristic of a positivist historical approach for this study, (5) the assumption that the individual is taken to be the ultimate object of study and the agent of historical change.

10. I would add to this observation that the widespread reliance on literal interpretations of the chronicles and the general acceptance of the traditional model of Inca state development provide few incentives for archaeological work in the Cuzco region on the development of the Inca state. The Spanish chronicles present rich images of the Chanca war, of the characters involved, and of Pachacuti Inca Yupanqui's legendary rise to political power. Archaeological data, on the other hand, are generally composed of cultural residues that have accumulated over time and are notoriously poor at illuminating single events of the past or the actions of specific individuals. If the elaborate details of the chronicles are accurate descriptions of the past and not mythical representations, and if the Inca state emerged in the Cuzco region as the direct result of Pachacuti Inca Yupanqui's "organizing genius," then archaeological investigations of state development in the Cuzco region are of limited value. Within an event-based perspective of historical change there is little need for archaeological research on Inca state formation, since the events can be "reconstructed" through (1) readings of the chronicles, (2) extracting so-called "historical facts" concerning the activities of Pachacuti Inca Yupanqui, and (3) placing the accounts within a "logical" chronological framework.

11. Since the mid-1980s the INC:Cuzco has been conducting a survey of the Cuzco Valley and other regions of the Department of Cuzco. Its completion and publication will mark an unprecedented contribution to Cuzco archaeology.

2. The Social Hierarchy of the Cuzco Region

1. It should be noted that the same name (Tambo, Tampus, Tanbo) is used in the Spanish chronicles to refer to two separate ethnic groups within the Cuzco region. One of these Tambo groups inhabited the Pacariqtambo region, to the south of Cuzco. The second Tambo group occupied the Ollantaytambo region northwest of Cuzco (Table 1).

2. As a prelude to the emergence of the four brothers and four sisters from the cave of Tambotoco, Guamán Poma de Ayala first describes Manco Capac and Mama Huaco leaving Lake Titicaca and walking to Tambotoco (Guamán Poma de Ayala [1615:80–85] 1980:63–65).

3. The chronicles are unanimous in reporting that the Inca nobility took their sons to the mountain of Huanacauri to have their ears pierced and ear-

spools inserted during the male initiation rite of Huaracikoy. The mountain of Huanacauri is located approximately 12 km to the south, southeast of Cuzco. As documented by Rowe (1944:41–43), a small set of ruins stands near the summit of the mountain, most likely marking the shrine of Huanacauri. The mountain of Huanacauri represented the northernmost point of our archaeological survey.

4. For additional discussions concerning hierarchical kinship models for the Cuzco region, see Zuidema (1983).

5. Guamán Poma de Ayala incorrectly places the Masca, Tambo, and Chillque groups in Collasuyu. As will be discussed, there is ample evidence to suggest that they were located directly south of Cuzco in Cuntisuyu (Poole 1984; Zuidema 1983).

6. See Zuidema (1977:278, 279).

7. After the formation of the Inca state, the Inca de Privilegio continued to play important roles in the organization of the empire. For example, it appears that they held a wide range of administrative positions throughout the newly conquered territories of the empire. Guamán Poma de Ayala presents a detailed discussion of administrative functions held by the Inca de Privilegio (Guamán Poma de Ayala [1615:346–363] 1980:318–335). While his list should not be interpreted literally as a description of state organization based on a series of highly specialized ethnic groups, it does emphasize the wide range of administrative positions that the various members of Inca de Privilegio groups could hold, including regional and provincial governors, judges, messengers, surveyors, administrators of the royal roads and bridges, and inspectors. Guamán Poma de Ayala specifically writes that the nobles from the Papri (Papres) and Chillque were frequently used as judges and inspectors of *tambos* (way stations), storehouses, and other installations of the empire (Guamán Poma de Ayala [1615:363] 1980:335).

Inca de Privilegio also appear to have played a critical role within Inca policies of colonization. After the conquest of a new region, the Inca frequently transferred part of the indigenous population of the region to a different area and brought colonists of differing ethnic backgrounds into the newly conquered province. Although the Inca institution of *mitmakuna* (colonist) is still little understood and demands an extensive study, it has become evident that Inca de Privilegio were frequently resettled in recently incorporated areas. Closely affiliated with the ruling social hierarchy in Cuzco and loyal to the Inca state, the Inca de Privilegio were ideal colonists. See Poole (1984) and Salas de Coloma (1979) for a discussion on the Chillque and Papres ethnic groups of the Paruro region and their role as mitmakuna near Vilcashuaman.

3. The Cuzco Chronology

1. A period of transformational crisis followed the execution of Atahualpa. For some forty years the Spaniards established and supported a series of puppet Inca kings in Cuzco. During this same period, the Spaniards also fought a protracted war against the descendants of Manco Inca (a half-brother of Atahualpa), who fled to the Vilcabamba region. The transitional period between

independent, indigenous rule in the Andes and Spanish control may be seen as ending in 1572 with the execution of Tupac Amaru Inca, the last surviving son of Manco Inca, and with the wide-scale implementation of the Spanish reducción policy under Viceroy Toledo.

2. See Rowe (1944:57, 61; 1945:275; 1946:199, 200, 203; 1957; 1970:561, 562; 1985:35), Brundage (1963:72), Rivera Dorado (1971a), Dwyer (1971:143), Gasparini and Margolies (1980:5), D'Altroy (1981:9), Julien (1982:121), Conrad and Demarest (1984:110), Kendall (1985:250), Patterson (1985:37), Niles (1987:7), Morris (1988:236), and Hyslop (1990:25).

3. All radiocarbon dates in this report are uncorrected. Calibration estimates have been provided using Stuiver and Reimer's (1986) Calib and Display programs. The ages and sigma (standard deviation) ranges have been obtained from intercepts using method A with no averaging. I have also used Stuiver and Reimer's (1986) notation for reporting the calibration estimates. In this notation the sigma range for a sample is presented on either side of two parentheses. The calibrated ages for the sample are presented between the parentheses.

4. Certain published radiocarbon dates from the Cuzco area have been excluded from Figures 4 and 5. For example, radiocarbon dates whose 1-sigma variances are so large as to render them useless (e.g., McEwan's Tx 4747 with a sigma of ±370) or samples that have provided dates well into the Colonial Period have not been included (see Kendall 1985:347; McEwan 1987:42–43, 89; Heffernan 1989:539).

All radiocarbon dates shown in Figures 4 and 5 contain correlated radiocarbon years (Stuiver and Reimer 1986). The exact intercepts for these samples, and their uncorrelated dates, are presented in Tables 3 and 4.

5. Two radiocarbon samples published by Kendall (1985:347) and McEwan (1987:80, 89) were collected from wall supports at the site of Choquepuquio, near Pikillacta. Currently, however, it is unclear whether the structures at Choquepuquio were built during the Huari occupation of the Cuzco Valley or in the period immediately following the abandonment of Pikillacta. The site of Choquepuquio contains Killke and Killke-related materials (Gibaja Oviedo 1973; McEwan 1983, 1984, 1987) as well as Huari and Inca materials. In addition, the two radiocarbon samples collected by Kendall and McEwan have yielded widely separated dates. Kendall's sample (BM 924) recorded a radiocarbon date of BP 695 ± 59 and a calibrated age of A.D. 1263 (1281) 1383. McEwan's sample (Tx 4748) provided a radiocarbon date of BP 1090 ± 60 and a calibrated date of A.D. 888 (979) 998. Since these two dates come from architectural features of uncertain cultural origin, their dates have not been included in this study.

6. Hollowell's sample SI 6986 from the site of Pumamarca has not been included in this discussion. Sample SI 6986 has a radiocarbon date of BP 940 ± 40 and a calibrated date of A.D. 1022 (1037, 1142, 1149) 1157. Three other samples from adjacent, and architecturally similar, buildings at the site of Pumamarca (SI 6987, SI 6988A, SI 6988B) provided closely matching ages, dating to 250 years later. I have accepted the three dates that cluster together to date the construction and not the single outlying date.

7. Also see Alcina Franch (1978) for dates from Ingapirca in Ecuador.

4. The Research Region and Research Methodology

1. For recent archaeological studies on the Inca in the Cuzco region see Rowe (1944), Dwyer (1971), Rivera Dorado (1971a, 1971b, 1972, 1973), Kendall (1974, 1976, 1985), Alcina Franch (1976), Alcina Franch et al. (1976), Gibaja Oviedo (1983, 1984), Niles (1980, 1987), Gonzales Corrales (1985), and Heffernan (1989).

2. I first visited the Province of Paruro in 1982. The region, long associated with the mythical origin of the Inca, seemed to have been neglected by other archaeologists, who had primarily concentrated their work either near the city of Cuzco or in the Vilcanota/Urubamba River Valley. At the time of my first visit, the only two Inca sites in the region known to archaeologists were Maukallaqta and Puma Orco. The ruins of Maukallaqta contain over 200 structures, as well as numerous examples of fine Inca stonework, including large double-jamb doorways, fountains, cobbled streets with drainage canals, and a ceremonial area surrounded by nine large triple-jamb niches (Chapter 7). Puma Orco, an elaborately carved rock outcrop close to Maukallaqta, is thought by many to represent the cave from which the mythical Manco Capac is said to have emerged (Muelle 1945; Pardo 1946; Bauer 1988, 1991; Urton 1989, 1990). After visiting these extraordinary Inca sites, I became interested in the functions of Maukallaqta and Puma Orco, the effects that these two installations had on the social and economic organization of the indigenous ethnic groups of the region, and the processes by which the ethnic groups of the Cuzco region were assimilated into the Inca state.

The formal fieldwork for the project began in 1984. During the first field season, systematic surveys were conducted in the districts of Pacariqtambo and Yaurisque, areas that were once controlled by the Masca and Tambo. Two weeks were also spent mapping the ruins of Maukallaqta and the structures at the base of Puma Orco (Bauer 1992). In 1985, the regional survey work was continued in the District of Yaurisque, between the village of Yaurisque and the Inca ruins of Huanacauri, and in the southern sectors of the District of Pacariqtambo. The survey was then extended to include most of the District of Paruro and the eastern edge of the District of Huanoquite. Late in the 1985 season, a reconnaissance trip was made from Huanoquite to Inca Pirca, a small Inca Period site overlooking the Apurimac River Valley. In 1986 the survey was extended into the region of the Chillque, south of the Apurimac River. The District of Colcha and parts of the districts of Accha and Pillpinto, as well as a small region around the remote town of Omacha, were surveyed. In addition, during the 1986 season three test pits were dug at the site of Acchakar, near the village of Pacariqtambo, and excavations were conducted at Maukallaqta. Most of the 1987 field season was dedicated to gaining more information on the ceramic sequence of the region. To this end, test excavations were conducted at sites in the districts of Yaurisque, Paruro, and Colcha. During the 1987 field season, most of the sites found in the previous three field seasons were revisited to check information recorded on the survey forms and a reconnaissance trip was made to the Inca Period site of Huacra Pucara in the Province of Acomayo. The majority of the laboratory work for the project took place in Cuzco during the rainy seasons of 1986 and 1987.

3. This is especially true of the area immediately south of the Apurimac River, near the communities of Colcha and Araypallpa.

4. This form of regional economic organization has been observed in other regions of the Department of Cuzco (Webster 1971, 1973; Yamamoto 1982) as well as elsewhere in the Andes (Murra 1972; Brush 1976, 1977; Guillet 1981).

5. See also Poole (1984:133).

6. *Panaca* refers to a noble lineage within the city of Cuzco.

7. It is interesting to note that in this representation of the Cuzco social order, a clear division is made between the inhabitants of Cuzco (the panacas of Yaura, China, Masca, and Quesco Ayllu) and the Inca de Privilegio, or what Molina calls "mitimaes" of the Cuzco region. The structure of Molina's representation is similar to those discussed in Chapter 2.

8. The Huarancalla bridge, located at a sharp curve in the Apurimac River, was one of several large suspension bridges built across the Apurimac River in the Cuzco region. The Peruvian geographer Antonio Raimondi crossed the bridge in the mid–nineteenth century:

> Pasé el Apurimac sobre un largo é inseguro puente de mimbres y subí en la banda opuesta al pueblo de Araypalpa que pertenece al distrito de Colcca. . . . (Raimondi 1874:228)

> I passed the Apurimac over a large and unstable wicker bridge and climbed up the opposite bank to the town of Araypallpa, which pertains to the District of Colcha. . . .

An iron cable suspension bridge remained at the site of Huarancalla until 1984, when the modern road from Paruro was extended across the river to reach Araypallpa and Colcha, and the suspension bridge was replaced by a highway bridge. The construction of the modern bridge has destroyed all evidence of the original suspension bridge footings. The bridge was most likely maintained during both the Killke and Inca periods by members of the various villages that surrounded it.

9. Urton reports that north of Pacariqtambo and south of Cuzco, this road is also called *Ankuq Ñan* (Urton 1984).

10. Leaders of survey crews included Melissa Baker, Tamara Bray, Silvia López Arangurí, Leslie Ranken, Nilo Torres Poblete, Wilbert Torres Poblete, and Wilbert Vera Robles.

11. The general state of site preservation in the Province of Paruro is not, however, as outstanding as in many other regions of the Andean highlands. For example, research reports from the Upper Mantaro region (Parsons and Hastings 1977; Earle et al. 1980) and the Huánuco Pampa region (Morris and Thompson 1985) describe Inca and pre-Inca sites with well-preserved stone masonry. In contrast, the majority of the Inca and pre-Inca sites in the Province of Paruro are represented only by dense concentrations of pottery fragments on the surface of plowed fields or on the sides of eroding ridges. Only a few of the archaeological sites in the region contain visible architectural remains. With the exception of the Inca installations of Maukallaqta, Puma Orco, and

Huanacauri, the ground plans of sites are not apparent from their surface remains. The lack of visible structural remains at most archaeological sites in the Province of Paruro suggests that the Killke and Inca period structures, like those of modern-day villages, were constructed of low stone foundation walls with adobe superstructures. These stone foundations have most likely either been buried in the centuries following the abandonment of the sites or had their stones removed for use in later constructions.

12. The availability of low-altitude aerial photographs and detailed topographic maps, essential tools in regional archaeological surveys, were important factors in the final selection of the Province of Paruro as a survey region. Unlike the situation for many locations in the Cuzco region, aerial photographs and topographic maps are available to the public for the Province of Paruro. Without these tools, systematic coverage of the research region would have been extremely difficult.

Aerial photographs of the research region are available at two locations: the Instituto Geográfico Militar (IGM) and the Servicio Aerofotográfico Nacional. The latter of these two institutions provides aerial photographs from two separate projects over the Province of Paruro. The first project (#8485) was conducted from March to April of 1956, and the second project (#287-77) was conducted from May to June of 1977. Complete sets of aerial photographs (25 by 25 cm) from both of these projects were purchased for reference use, while selected photographs were enlarged to prints 1 m by 1 m (ground scale approximately 1:10,000) for use during the actual survey. The 1977 project photographs were amplified because of their greater resolution.

Contour maps of the region are available from two sources. The IGM has 1:100,000 as well as 1:25,000 maps of the Province of Paruro with 50-m contours. The IGM also produces a 1:747,000 map of the Department of Cuzco. The Ministerio de Agricultura also has 1:25,000 maps of the Province of Paruro; however, these have a contour interval of 25 m. During the course of the project the 1:25,000 Ministerio de Agricultura maps were used in the field to mark the location and boundaries of sites, while the larger-scale 1:100,000 IGM maps were used to examine the region's relationship with Cuzco and more distant territories.

13. While surveying in high environmental zones for evidence of prehistoric occupation and land use, the surveyors assisting in this research frequently had to deviate from their survey lines to examine stream cuts or to inspect scattered patches of earth where the grass had eroded away and the soil was exposed.

The sites in the puna area, which generally were composed of circular stone corrals, were especially difficult to date because they were frequently covered by thick grass. Even in cases where corrals were currently being used for potato cultivation and there was good ground visibility, the sites yielded very little pottery. Ethnographic observations help to explain the difficulty in recovering artifacts at these sites. Contemporary use of high-altitude corrals in the Province of Paruro is limited to the wet season, which lasts approximately from November through April. During his brief stay at the corrals, the modern herder will use a bare minimum of domestic items. This combination of short-term occupation, limited use of ceramic vessels, and thick grass coverage frequently makes period identification of puna sites difficult.

14. Certain aspects of archaeological work in the Province of Paruro were also complicated by the conservative nature of the rural population. The general isolation of the area encouraged misunderstandings between researchers and the local population. Occasionally the scientific nature of the project was not understood and surveyors were accused of being either terrorists or gold prospectors. These problems were further complicated by our inability to express ourselves as clearly as we would have liked in several of the Quechua-speaking communities. While good relationships were established between the project and most of the communities in the region, one set of test excavations was ended near the village of Pacariqtambo because of local concerns.

15. At the close of the Pacariqtambo Archaeological Project, all artifacts were deposited in the INC:Cuzco.

16. The surface collections from the sites in the Province of Paruro document the existence of every known pottery style so far recorded in the Cuzco Valley. These include Classic Inca, with types A, B, and Collasuyu (Rowe 1944); Early Inca or Killke (Rowe 1944; Dwyer 1971); Qotakalli (Middle Horizon) (Barreda Murillo 1982); Huari (Middle Horizon) (McEwan 1983, 1987); Araway (Middle Horizon) (Torres Poblete 1989); and Derived Chanapata (Early Intermediate) (Rowe 1944, 1956; Chávez 1980, 1981a, 1981b; Yábar Moreno 1972, 1982), as well as Chanapata and Marcavalle (Early Horizon) (Rowe 1944; Chávez 1980, 1981a, 1981b). Three new and widespread styles were also found in the region of investigation and have been named Muyu Orco, Ccoipa, and Colcha. The first two of these ceramic styles appear to represent pre-Killke Period ceramic styles. Ccoipa pottery may represent an Early Intermediate or Middle Horizon ceramic tradition, while Muyu Orco pottery appears to reflect a Tiahuanaco influence in the Cuzco region (Bauer 1990b). These ceramic styles are currently under study and will be discussed in a separate work. The third new ceramic style, Colcha, is stylistically similar to Killke pottery, and is discussed in Chapter 5.

17. Elliana Gamarra Carrillo and Marlene Pinares helped to supervise the processing of the artifact collections in Cuzco.

5. Killke Period Pottery Production and Exchange in the Cuzco Region

1. Sections of this chapter have appeared in Bauer and Stanish (1990). They are reprinted here with permission from the Field Museum of Natural History.

2. In this book, only the decorated shards of these ceramic types are discussed. Additional research is needed before the undecorated shards can be described.

3. The pottery style found by Rowe in his excavations in the monastery of Santo Domingo was first named "Canchon" (Rowe 1944:46). After his 1942–43 fieldwork in Cuzco, Rowe renamed the new pottery style "Killke" after a site located on the outskirts of the city (Rowe 1944:60–61).

4. Recent radiocarbon-14 dates suggest that Killke pottery may have been produced in the Cuzco region as early as A.D. 1000 and continued until approximately A.D. 1400 (see Chapter 3).

5. The calibrated date of this sample is set at A.D. 1069 (1261) 1385 (see Chapter 3).

6. The earliest reference I have found to the site comes from a 1647 document that uses the ridge as a boundary marker:

> Una peña grande que mira al dicho pueblo [Paruro] nombrada Texaquaci. (ADC, Tesorería Fiscal, Libros de Colegios, 1647, No. 1, f. 129)

> A large ridge that overlooks the said town [Paruro] named Tejahuasi.

7. Huari pottery was found at nine sites in the research region during our surface collections. In 1987, test excavations were conducted at a single-component Huari site near Paruro. The Huari pottery recovered is similar to that found by McEwan (1983, 1987) during his excavations at the Huari complex of Pikillacta, six hours by trail from the Paruro Valley, in the Lucre basin. These collections will be analyzed in a separate study.

Chávez (1985) also reports that two fragments of Early Tiahuanaco-related ceremonial burners were found at Tejahuasi.

8. Sample B 27494.

9. Tejahuasi most likely represents the pre-reducción location of ayllu Cucuchiráy, which, like eleven other ayllus in the immediate area, was resettled into the town of Paruro in 1571 during the reducción policy of Viceroy Toledo (Ulloa 1909:334).

10. The statistical analyses conducted in this section are based on the systematic regional survey data collected in the Province of Paruro from 1984 to 1987. For the methodology of the survey see Chapter 4. Pottery dating to the Killke Period was found in 102 sites. Of these sites, 56 contained Killke pottery and 79 Colcha pottery. Both Killke and Colcha pottery were found in 33 of the 102 sites.

11. Because many of the Killke Period sites in the Province of Paruro are small and yielded limited collections of surface pottery, I have elected to use a "presence/absence" measure of Killke and Colcha pottery in this study, rather than to discuss the relative quantities of these ceramic types (or specific attributes) present at each site. Thus, until additional research is conducted in the region, including a large-scale excavation program at a number of different sites and an expanded program of surface collections, these results should be considered as provisional.

12. Because a study of the modern pottery production in Araypallpa is planned for the future, only a summary will be presented here. As in many Andean communities (Arnold 1972, 1975, 1985; Chávez 1984; O'Neale 1977), there are no full-time potters in the village of Araypallpa. Most of the pottery is produced by women during the dry season. The clay for the vessels is extracted from several deposits immediately to the south of the town. The festival of El Señor de Pampacucho, traditionally held each year on 16 August in

the community of Pampacucho, 8 km south of Araypallpa, used to be an important festival for the exchange of pottery and produce in the region. However, with the general decline of the festival over the past decade, this is no longer the case. Currently, the products of the individual potters of the village are carried to the towns of Paruro or Accha to be traded or sold at the Sunday markets.

13. Poole, during her ethnographic studies in Paruro and Colcha, discussed another vessel produced in the village of Araypallpa that is still widely used in the Paruro region during festivals. She describes this vessel as "a round, unpainted ceramic bowl with one very small handle, manufactured only in the community of Araypallpa, and used only during August and Carnival" (1984:293). When Poole asked why the vessel was called "Chillque" (or "Ch'ellqe"), she was told, "Because it was made in Araypallpa" (1984:468).

14. Luis Barreda Murillo recovered two nearly complete Colcha vessels during excavations at the site of Wimpillay on the edge of the city of Cuzco (Barreda Murillo pers. com. 1990).

15. It is possible that certain Chillque or Inca potters (if ethnographic analogies are correct, women) may have relocated during the period of state formation as part of marriage alliances between the various ethnic groups.

16. I have assumed here that the ethnic groups of the Cuzco region, whom the Inca called Inca de Privilegio, were indigenous to the Cuzco region and occupied approximately the same regions during both the Killke and Inca periods. In the following chapter, extensive subsistence-settlement evidence indicating a continuous and uninterrupted occupation of the Province of Paruro from the Killke Period to the Inca Period is presented to support this assumption.

17. For other examples see Bauer (1990a, App. I: Figs. 45, 46, 47), as well as Seler (1893: Lam. 6, Fig. 6), Jijón y Caamaño (1934: Fig. 54), Dwyer (1971, Figs. 291, 292), and Bauer and Stanish (1990: Figs. 5, 6, 11, 15, 16).

6. The Subsistence-Settlement Systems of the Province of Paruro during the Killke and Inca Periods

1. The boundaries of these survey regions do not, except in the case of Pacariqtambo, correspond with the exact boundaries of the modern political districts of the same name. See Bauer (1990a:104–117) for a detailed description of the Pacariqtambo, Yaurisque, Paruro, and Colcha areas and the distribution of their Killke and Inca period sites.

2. See Webster (1971, 1973), Brush (1976, 1977), Guillet (1981), and Yamamoto (1982) for ethnographic studies of modern, vertically based village economies in the Andes.

3. The exact pattern in which the sites were distributed across the landscape in each of the regions appears to differ, however, in relation to the specific ecological properties of the region. For example, in the agriculturally poor region of Colcha the small sites are tightly clustered in the lower elevations of the Apurimac River Valley between 3,000 and 3,200 masl, while in the region of Pacariqtambo the smaller sites are uniformly distributed across a wide range of elevations between 2,850 and 3,825 masl (Bauer 1990a).

4. See Chapter 7 for a continued discussion of Maukallaqta and Puma Orco.

5. See also the discussion of the Late Intermediate Period by Parsons and Hastings (1988).

6. Heffernan uses the term *LPT* or Late Prehistoric Tradition in place of Killke Period.

7. Maukallaqta and Puma Orco

1. Sections of this chapter have appeared in Bauer (1991, 1992). They are reprinted here by permission of the Society for American Archaeology (copyright 1991) and Ñawpa Pacha (copyright 1992).

2. As you stand in the gateway to zone 2 and look across the Huaynacancha Quebrada, the carved stone outcrop of Puma Orco is within your field of vision.

3. The depth of occupation at the site will remain unknown until excavations are conducted.

4. For a review of earlier archaeological work at the site by Bingham (1913, 1922), Muelle (1945), Pardo (1946), and Kendall (1985), see Bauer (1990a, 1991, 1992).

5. The 1986 excavations at Maukallaqta are discussed in detail in Bauer (1990a, 1992).

6. The extraction and storage of surplus production in provincial centers by the Inca have been examined in a number of studies (Morris 1967; Earle et al. 1980; D'Altroy 1981; Earle and D'Altroy 1982; D'Altroy and Earle 1985; D'Altroy and Hastorf 1984; LeVine 1985).

7. See LeVine (1985) for an analysis of Inca administration in the regions of Huánuco Pampa, Hatun Xauxa, and Pumpu.

8. In a work closely related to this chapter, I trace the mythical journey of Manco Capac and his royal siblings from this outcrop to the Cuzco Valley (Bauer 1991). See also Urton (1989, 1990) for a detailed examination of the myth from the perspective of the rural community of Pacariqtambo.

8. The Ayllu and Moiety Organizations of the Tambo Ethnic Group during the Killke and Inca Periods

1. The Tambo ethnic group, which inhabited the Pacariqtambo region, was selected for this case study because it represents the regional Cuzco ethnic group for which we have the most detailed ethnographic and ethnohistorical information. This information is largely the result of Urton's work in the Pacariqtambo region (1984, 1985, 1986, 1988, 1989, 1990).

Although my archaeological research in the Pacariqtambo region was conducted independently of Urton's ethnographic and ethnohistorical work, he allowed me access to numerous archival documents in his possession and to several of his unpublished manuscripts. Without this generous sharing of information, the analysis in this chapter could not have been completed.

2. Relatively few Andean archaeologists have attempted to include indigenous conceptions of dual social organization in their interpretation of site remains and settlement patterns (notable exceptions include Dillehay 1976, 1979; Netherly 1984; Netherly and Dillehay 1986; and Anders 1986, among others). As emphasized by Anders (1986:723), the failure to interpret Andean archaeological remains through models of dual social organization "has less to do with the lack of evidence than with the shortsightedness caused by researchers' ideological commitments to occidental based models of social and economic organization which do not accommodate dual principles of organization."

3. During this forced resettlement program, begun under Viceroy Toledo in 1571, many of the indigenous settlements of the central Andes were destroyed and the majority of the population was resettled into large, newly constructed communities.

4. Gade and Escobar Moscoso (1982) provide a detailed study of the reducciones established by the Spaniards in the Paruro region and factors related to the eventual abandonment of many of these centers.

5. Near the end of the 1571 document, the repartimiento of San Pedro de Pacariqtambo is listed as containing only ten pueblos viejos (Ulloa 1909:342).

6. For the purpose of this work the term *ayllu* is defined as a small, internally autonomous kin group that communally owned and worked a specific territory. As such they represent the segmentary units of rural organization and of Inca society.

7. An excerpt from the 1568 document was sent by Luis Miguel Glave to Gary Urton (1989:188; 1990:146). Urton (1988 pers. com.) provided me with a copy of the excerpt.

8. It is interesting to note in the 1568 document that leaders from most of the hanansaya ayllus (four out of five) attended the meeting. This large percentage stands in contrast to the relatively poor representation of the hurinsaya ayllus at the meeting (two out of six). The different attendance of the hanansaya and hurinsaya ayllus perhaps reflects a reluctance of the lower moiety to formally appoint a single leader for the repartimiento.

9. Urton (1988, 1990) presents an expanded version of this table, extending the ayllu and moiety divisions up to the present day.

10. Cuño disappears from the Pacariqtambo ayllu lists during the same period in which ayllu San Miguel appears, suggesting that they may represent the same ayllu under different names.

11. It is possible that the pre-reducción location of ayllu Cuño/San Miguel is a small ridge called Jurinka, which is traditionally thought to be the origin point for ayllu Pirca. I favor this location as the original settlement place of San Miguel, since the 1594 document for the region lists the ayllu of San Miguel as the owner of land at Jurinka.

12. The names of these sites are Maukallaqta (I), Ayusbamba (II), Ayapata (III), Pirca Moco (IV), and Huichuro (V).

13. Given Site IV's close proximity to the modern-day community of Pirca and its location on a ridge called Pirca Moco (Pirca Mountain), it is possible

Bibliography

Primary Sources

Archivo Departamental del Cuzco, Cuzco (ADC) Tesorería Fiscal, Libros de Colegios, No. 1, 1647.
Archivo del Ministerio de Agricultura: Cuzco (AMAC) Expediente #5877, 1944. Expediente #4281, 1964.

Secondary Sources

Acosta, José de
    1954   Historia natural y moral de las Indias [1590]. *Biblioteca de autores españoles* (continuación), vol. 73. Madrid: Ediciones Atlas.
Albornoz, Cristóbal de
    1967   La instrucción para descubrir todas las guacas del Pirú y sus camayos y haziendas [c. 1582]. *Journal de la Société des Américanistes* [edited by Pierre Duviols] 56 (1): 7–39.
Alcina Franch, José
    1976   *Arqueología de Chinchero: La arquitectura*, vol. 2, *Memorias de la misión científica española en Hispanoamérica*. Madrid: Ministerio de Asuntos Exteriores.
Alcina Franch, José
    1978   Ingapirca: Arquitectura y áreas de asentamiento. *Revista española de antropología americana* (Trabajos y Conferencias), pp. 127–146. Madrid: Facultad de Geografía e Historia, Universidad Complutense.
Alcina Franch, J., M. Rivera, J. Galvan, C. Garcia Palacios, M. Guinea, B. Martinez-Caviro, L. J. Ramos, and T. Varela
    1976   *Arqueología de Chinchero: Cerámica y otros materiales*, vol. 3, *Memorias de la misión científica española en Hispanoamérica*. Madrid: Ministerio de Asuntos Exteriores.

Ammerman, Albert J.

1981   Surveys and archaeological research. *Annual Review of Anthropology* 10:63–88.

Anders, Martha B.

1986   *Dual organization and calendars inferred from the planned site of Azángaro-Wari administrative strategies.* Ann Arbor, Mich.: University Microfilms.

Arnold, Dean E.

1972   Native pottery making in Quinua, Peru. *Anthropos* 67:858–872

1975   Ceramic ecology of the Ayacucho Basin, Peru: Implications for prehistory. *Current Anthropology* 16 (2): 183–205.

1980   Localized exchange: An ethnoarchaeological perspective. In *Models and methods in regional exchange.* Edited by R. E. Fry, pp. 147–150. SAA Papers 1. Washington, D.C.: Society for American Archaeology.

1985   *Ceramic theory and cultural process.* Cambridge, England: Cambridge University Press.

Baca Cosio, Jenaro F.

1974   *Motivos de ornamentación de la cerámica inca Cusco (Tomo I).* Camaná, Peru: Librería Studium S. A.

1989   *Motivos de ornamentación de la cerámica inca Cusco (Tomo II).* Camaná, Peru: Librería Studium S. A.

Barreda Murillo, Luis

1973   Las culturas inka y pre-inka de Cuzco. Tesis, Department of Archaeology, University of San Antonio Abad, Cuzco.

1982   Asentamiento humano de los Qotakalli del Cuzco. In *Arqueología de Cuzco.* Compiled by Italo Oberti Rodríguez, pp. 13–21. Cuzco: Instituto Nacional de Cultura.

Bauer, Brian S.

1987   Sistemas andinos de organizacíon rural antes del establecimiento de reducciones: El ejemplo de Pacariqtambo (Perú). *Revista andina* 9 (1): 197–210.

1988   Pacariqtambo and the mythical origins of the Incas. Paper presented at the 46th International Congress of Americanists, Amsterdam.

1990a   State development in the Cusco region: Archaeological research on the Incas in the Province of Paruro. Ph.D. diss., Department of Anthropology, University of Chicago.

1990b   Muyu Orqo y Ccoipa: Dos nuevos tipos de cerámica para la región del Cusco. *Revista andina* 7 (2): 537–542.

1991   Pacariqtambo and the mythical origins of the Inca. *Latin American Antiquity* 2:7–26.

1992   Recent archaeological investigations at the sites of Maukallaqta and Puma Orco, Department of Cuzco, Peru. *Ñawpa Pacha.* Forthcoming.

Bauer, Brian S., and Charles Stanish

1990   Killke and Killke-related pottery from Cuzco, Peru, in the Field Museum of Natural History. *Fieldiana.* Anthropology Series no. 15. Chicago: Field Museum of Natural History.

Betanzos, Juan de
  1987   *Suma y narración de los Incas* [1551]. Edited by Maria del Carmen
          Martin Rubio. Madrid: Ediciones Atlas.
Bingham, Hiram
  1910   The ruins of Choqquequirau. *American Anthropologist* 12:505–525.
  1913   In the wonderlands of Peru: The work accomplished by the Peruvian
          Expedition of 1912. *National Geographic Magazine* 24:387–573.
  1915a   The story of Machu Picchu: The National Geographic Society–Yale
          University explorations in Peru. *National Geographic Magazine*
          27:172–186, 203–217.
  1915b   Types of Machu Picchu pottery. *American Anthropologist* 17 (2):
          257–271.
  1922   *Inca land: Explorations in the highlands of Peru.* Cambridge, Mass.:
          Riverside Press.
  1930   *Machu Picchu: A citadel of the Incas.* New Haven: National Geo-
          graphic Society and Yale University Press.
Bouysse-Cassagne, Thérèse
  1986   Urco and uma: Aymara concepts of space. In *Anthropological his-
          tory of Andean polities.* Ed. J. V. Murra, N. Wachtel, and J. Revel,
          pp. 201–227. Cambridge: Cambridge University Press.
Browman, David L.
  1970   Early Peruvian peasants: The culture history of a central highlands
          valley. Ph.D. diss., Department of Anthropology, Harvard University.
Brundage, Burr C.
  1963   *Empire of the Inca.* Norman: University of Oklahoma Press.
  1967   *Lords of Cuzco: A history and description of the Inca people in
          their final days.* Norman: University of Oklahoma Press.
Brush, Stephen B.
  1976   Man's use of an Andean ecosystem. *Human Ecology* 4 (2): 147–166.
  1977   *Mountain, field, and family: The economy and human ecology of
          an Andean village.* Philadelphia: University of Pennsylvania Press.
Burger, Richard L.
  1989   An overview of Peruvian archaeology (1976–1986). *Annual Review
          of Anthropology* 18:37–69.
Cabello Balboa, Miguel
  1951   *Miscelánea antártica; una historia del Peru antiguo* [1586]. Edited
          by L. E. Valcárcel. Lima: Universidad Nacional Mayor de San Mar-
          cos, Instituto de Etnología.
Capoche, Luis
  1959   Relación general de la villa imperial de Potosí, un capítulo inedito
          en la historia del nuevo mundo [1585]. Prólogo y notas de Lewis
          Hanke. *Biblioteca de autores españoles* (continuación), vol. 122, pp.
          9–221. Madrid: Ediciones Atlas.
Chávez, Karen L. M.
  1980   The archaeology of Marcavalle, an Early Horizon site in the Valley
          of Cuzco, Peru: Part I. *Baessler-Archiv,* neue Folge, 28 (2): 203–329.

1981a The archaeology of Marcavalle, an Early Horizon site in the Valley of Cuzco, Peru: Part II. *Baessler-Archiv, neue Folge,* 29 (1): 107–205.

1981b The archaeology of Marcavalle, an Early Horizon site in the Valley of Cuzco, Peru: Part III. *Baessler-Archiv, neue Folge,* 29 (1): 241–386.

1984 Traditional pottery of Raqch'i, Cusco, Peru: A preliminary study of its production, distribution, and consumption. *Ñawpa Pacha* 22–23:161–210.

1985 Early Tiahuanaco-related ceremonial burners from Cuzco, Peru. In *Diálogo andino no.* 4, pp. 137–178. Arica, Chile: Departamento de Historia y Geografía, Universidad de Tarapacá.

Cieza de León, Pedro de

1959 *The Incas of Pedro Cieza de León* [1553]. Translated by Harriet de Onís and edited by Victor W. von Hagen. Norman: University of Oklahoma Press.

1985 *La crónica del Perú* [1553]. Edited by Manuel Ballesteros. Madrid: Historia 16.

Cobo, Bernabé

1956 Historia del Nuevo Mundo [1653]. *Biblioteca de autores españoles* (continuación), vol. 92. Madrid: Ediciones Atlas.

1979 *History of the Inca Empire: An account of the Indians' customs and their origin together with a treatise on Inca legends, history, and social institutions* [1653]. Translated and edited by Roland Hamilton. Austin: University of Texas Press.

Cohen, Ronald

1978 State origins: A reappraisal. In *The early state.* Edited by H. J. M. Claessen and P. Skalnik, pp. 31–75. The Hague: Mouton.

Collier, George A., Renato I. Rosaldo, and John D. Wirth, eds.

1982 *The Inca and Aztec states, 1400–1800: Anthropology and history.* New York: Academic Press.

Conrad, Geoffrey W.

1981 Cultural materialism, split inheritance, and the expansion of ancient Peruvian empires. *American Antiquity* 46 (1): 2–26.

Conrad, Geoffrey W., and Arthur A. Demarest

1984 *Religion and empire: The dynamics of Aztec and Inca expansionism.* Cambridge: Cambridge University Press.

Conrad, Geoffrey W., and Ann Webster

1989 Household unit patterning at San Antonio. In *Ecology, settlement and history in the Osmore Drainage, southern Peru,* parts 1 and 2. Edited by Don S. Rice, Charles Stanish, and Phillip R. Scarr. BAR International Series 545, *British Archaeological Reports,* Oxford, England.

D'Altroy, Terence N.

1981 *Empire growth and consolidation: The Xauxa region of Peru under the Incas.* Ann Arbor, Mich.: University Microfilms.

1987a Introduction. *Ethnohistory* 34 (1): 1–13.

1987b   Transitions in power: Centralization of Wanka political organization under Inka rule. *Ethnohistory* 34 (1): 78–102.

D'Altroy, Terence N., and Timothy K. Earle
1985   Staple finance, wealth finance, and storage in the Inka political economy (including comment and replay). *Current Anthropology* 25 (2): 187–206.

D'Altroy, Terence N., and Christine A. Hastorf
1984   The distribution and contents of Inca state storehouses in the Xauxa region of Peru. *American Antiquity* 49 (2): 334–349.

Decoster, Jean-Jacques
1989   Dualidad andina: Estructura social y transformación (Accha siglos XVI–XX). Paper presented at Centro de Estudios Rurales Andinos, "Bartolomé de Las Casas," Cuzco.

Demarest, Arthur A., and Geoffrey W. Conrad
1983   Ideological adaptation and the rise of the Aztec and Inca empires. In *Civilization in the ancient Americas: Essays in honor of Gordon R. Willey*. Edited by R. M. Leventhal and A. L. Kolata, pp. 373–400. Albuquerque: University of New Mexico Press.

Diez de San Miguel, Garci
1964   Visita hecha a la provincia de Chucuito por Garci Diez de San Miguel en el año 1567. *Documentos regionales para la etnología y etnohistoria andina* (Tomo 1). Lima: Casa de la Cultura del Peru.

Dillehay, Tom
1976   Competition and cooperation in a pre-Hispanic multi-ethnic system in the Central Andes. Ph.D. diss., Department of Anthropology, University of Texas, Austin.
1977   Tawantinsuyu integration of the Chillón Valley, Peru: A case of Inca geo-political mastery. *Journal of Field Archaeology* 4 (4): 397–405.
1979   Pre-Hispanic resource sharing in the central Andes. *Science* 204 (6): 24–31.

Duviols, Pierre
1979a   La guerra entre el Cuzco y los Chanca: Historia o mito? *Revista de la Universidad Complutense* 28 (117): 263–271.
1979b   La dinastía de los Incas: Monarquía o diarquía? *Journal de la Société des Américanistes* 66:67–83.

Dwyer, Edward B.
1971   The Early Inca occupation of the Valley of Cuzco, Peru. Ph.D. diss., Department of Anthropology, University of California, Berkeley.

Earle, Timothy K., and Terence N. D'Altroy
1982   Storage facilities and state finance in the Upper Mantaro Valley, Peru. In *Contexts for prehistoric exchange*. Edited by J. E. Ericson and T. K. Earle, pp. 265–290. New York: Academic Press.

Earle, Timothy K., Terence N. D'Altroy, Christine A. Hastorf, Catherine Scott, Cathy L. Costin, Glenn S. Russell, and Elsie Sandefur
1988   *Investigations of Inka expansion and exchange.* Monograph 28. Los Angeles: Institute of Archaeology, University of California.

Earle, Timothy K., Terence N. D'Altroy, Catherine J. LeBlanc, Christine A. Hastorf, and Terry Y. LeVine

1980   Changing settlement patterns in the Upper Mantaro Valley, Peru. *Journal of New World Archaeology* 4:1–49.

Eaton, George F.

1914   Vertebrate fossils from Ayusbamba, Peru. *American Journal of Science*, 4th ser., 37 (218): 141–154.

1916   The collection of osteological material from Machu Picchu. *Memoirs of the Connecticut Academy of Arts and Sciences* 5:3–96.

Engel, Frédéric

1966   *Geografía humana prehistórica y agricultura precolombina de la Quebrada de Chilca* (Tomo 1). Lima: Universidad Agraria.

Escobar Moscoso, Mario

1980   Estudio comparativo de los Valles de Urubamba y el Apurimac. In *Actas y trabajos del III congreso peruano "El Hombre y la cultura andina"* (Tomo 4), pp. 657–674. Lima: Universidad Nacional Mayor de San Marcos.

Espinoza Soriano, Waldemar

1973   *La destrucción de la conquista.* Lima: Retablo de Papel Ediciones.

1977   Los cuatro suyos del Cuzco, siglos XV y XVI. *Bulletin de l'Institut Français des Études Andines* 6 (3–4): 109–122.

Fejos, Paul

1944   *Archaeological explorations in the Cordillera Vilcabamba.* New York: Viking Fund Publications in Anthropology.

Flannery, Kent V.

1972   The cultural evolution of civilizations. *Annual Review of Ecology and Systematics* 3:399–426.

Fogelson, Raymond D.

1989   The ethnohistory of events and nonevents. *Ethnohistory* 36 (2): 133–147.

Franco Inojosa, José M., and Luis A. Llanos

1940   Trabajos arqueológicos en el Dep. del Cusco. Sajsawaman. Una excavación en el edificio de Muyumarca. *Revista del Museo Nacional* 9 (1): 22–32.

Fré.zier, Amédée François

1732   *Relation du voyage de la mer du Sud aux côtes du Chily et du Pérou fait pendant les années 1712, 1713, & 1714* [1716]. Paris: Chez Nyon . . . , Chez Didot . . . , Chez Quillau. . . .

Gade, Daniel W.

1966   Achira, the edible canna: Its cultivation and use in the Peruvian Andes. *Economic Botany* 22:407–414.

1975   *Plants, man and the land in the Vilcanota Valley of Peru.* The Hague: Dr. W. Junk B. V.

Gade, Daniel W., and Mario Escobar Moscoso

1982   Village settlement and the colonial legacy in southern Peru. *Geographical Review* 72 (4): 430–449.

Garcilaso de la Vega, Inca
1945   Los comentarios reales de los Incas [1609]. Edited by Ricardo Rojas. Buenos Aires: Emecé Editores, S. A.
1966   Royal commentaries of the Incas and general history of Peru, parts 1 and 2 [1609]. Translated by H. V. Livermore. Austin: University of Texas Press.

Gasparini, Graziano, and Luise Margolies
1980   Inca architecture. Translated by P. J. Lyon. Bloomington: Indiana University Press.

Gibaja Oviedo, Arminda M.
1973   Arqueología de Choquepugio. Tesis, Department of Archaeology, University of San Antonio Abad, Cuzco.
1983   Arqueología de Choquepugio. In Arqueología andina, Asociación de arqueología andina, pp. 29–44. Cuzco: Ediciones Instituto Nacional de Cultura.
1984   Sequencia cultural de Ollantaytambo. In Current archaeological projects in the central Andes. Edited by A. Kendall, pp. 225–246. BAR International Series 210, British Archaeological Reports, Oxford, England.

Gonzales Corrales, José
1985   La arquitectura y cerámica killke del Cusco. In Current archaeological projects in the central Andes. Edited by A. Kendall, pp. 189–204. BAR International Series 210, British Archaeological Reports, Oxford, England.

Gregory, Herbert E.
1914   Geologic reconnaissance of the Ayusbamba fossil beds. American Journal of Science, 4th ser., 37 (218): 125–140.

Guaman Poma de Ayala, Felipe
1980   El primer nueva corónica y buen gobierno [1584–1615]. Edited by J. V. Murra and R. Adorno, and translated by Jorge I. Urioste. 3 vols. Mexico City: Siglo Veintiuno.

Guillet, David
1981   Land tenure, agricultural regime, and ecological zones in the central Andes. American Ethnologist 8 (1): 19–28.

Hastorf, Christine A.
1983   Prehistoric agricultural intensification and political development in the Jauja Region of central Peru. Ann Arbor, Mich.: University Microfilms.

Heffernan, Kenneth J.
1989   Limatambo in late prehistory: Landscape archaeology and documentary images of Inca presence in the periphery of Cusco. Ph.D. diss., Department of Prehistory and Anthropology, Australian National University, Canberra.

Hemming, John
1970   The conquest of the Incas. New York: Harcourt Brace Jovanovich.

Hodder, Ian
1974   Regression analysis of some trade and marketing patterns. World Archaeology 6 (2): 172–189.

1980   Trade and exchange: Definitions, identification and function. In *Models and methods in regional exchange.* Edited by R. E. Fry, pp. 151–156. SAA Papers 1. Washington, D.C.: Society for American Archaeology.

Hodder, Ian, and Colin G. Orton

1976   *Spatial analysis in archaeology.* Cambridge: Cambridge University Press.

Hollowell, J. Lee

1987   Precision cutting and fitting of stone in prehistoric Andean walls. Unpublished Research Report #2832–84, submitted to the National Geographic Society, Washington, D.C.

1989   Reassessment of the Fortaleza, Ollantaytambo, Peru. Paper presented at the 54th Annual Meeting of the Society for American Archaeology, 5–9 April, Atlanta, Ga.

Hutterer, Karl L., and William K. Macdonald

1982   *Houses built on scattered poles: Prehistory and ecology in Negros Oriental.* Cebu City, Philippines: University of San Carlos.

Hyslop, John, Jr.

1976   *An archaeological investigation of the Lupaca kingdom and its origins.* Ann Arbor, Mich.: University Microfilms.

1984   *The Inca road system.* New York: Academic Press.

1990   *Inka settlement planning.* Austin: University of Texas Press.

Isbell, William H.

1978   Environmental perturbations and the origin of the Andean state. In *Social archaeology.* Edited by C. Redman et al., pp. 303–314. New York: Academic Press.

Isbell, William H., and Katharina J. Schreiber

1978   Was Huari a state? *American Antiquity* 43:372–389.

Jijón y Caamaño, Jacinto

1934   *Los orígenes del Cuzco.* Quito: Imprenta de la Universidad Central.

Jijón y Caamaño, Jacinto, and Carlos Larrea M.

1918   Un cementerio incaico en Quito y notas acerca de los Incas en el Ecuador. *Revista de la Sociedad Jurídico-Literaria* 20:159–260.

Julien, Catherine J.

1978   *Inca administration in the Titicaca Basin as reflected at the provincial capital of Hatunqolla.* Ann Arbor, Mich.: University Microfilms.

1982   Inca decimal administration in the Lake Titicaca region. In *The Inca and Aztec states, 1400–1800: Anthropology and history.* Edited by G. Collier et al., pp. 119–151. New York: Academic Press.

1983   *Hatunqolla: A view of Inca rule from the Lake Titicaca region.* Berkeley and Los Angeles: University of California Press.

Keatinge, Richard W., ed.

1988   *Peruvian prehistory.* Cambridge: Cambridge University Press.

Kendall, E. Ann

1974   *Aspects of Inca architecture.* Ph.D. diss., Institute of Archaeology, University of London.

1976   Preliminary report on ceramic data and the pre-Inca architectural remains of the (Lower) Urubamba Valley, Cuzco. *Baessler Archiv, neue Folge*, Band 24:41–159.

1985   *Aspects of Inca architecture: Description, function and chronology, parts 1 and 2.* BAR International Series 242, British Archaeological Reports, Oxford, England.

LeBlanc, Catherine J.

1981   *Late prehispanic Huanca settlement patterns in the Yanamarca Valley, Peru.* Ann Arbor, Mich.: University Microfilms.

LeVine, Terry Y.

1985   *Inka administration in the central highlands: A comparative study.* Ann Arbor, Mich.: University Microfilms.

1987   Inka labor service at the regional level: The functional reality. *Ethnohistory* 34 (1): 14–46.

Llanos, Luis A.

1936   Trabajos arqueológicos en el Departamento del Cuzco bajo la dirección del Dr. Luis E. Valcárcel. Informe sobre Ollantaytambo. *Revista del Museo Nacional* 5 (2): 123–156.

Lumbreras, Luis G.

1978   Acerca de la aparición del estado inka. In *Actas y trabajos del III congreso peruano "El hombre y la cultura andina"* (Tomo 1). Edited by R. Matos M., pp. 101–109. Lima: Universidad Nacional Mayor de San Marcos.

Lunt, Sara W.

1983   An introduction to the pottery from the excavations at Cusichaca, Department of Cuzco. Paper presented at the 44th Meeting of the International Congress of Americanists, Manchester, England.

1987   Inca and pre-Inca pottery: Pottery from Cusichaca, Department of Cuzco, Peru. Ph.D. diss., Institute of Archaeology, University of London.

MacCurdy, George G.

1923   Human skeletal remains from the highlands of Peru. *American Journal of Physical Anthropology* 6 (3): 217–329.

McEwan, Gordon F.

1983   The Middle Horizon in the Valley of Cuzco, Peru: The impact of the Wari occupation of Pikillacta in the Lucre Basin. Ph.D diss., Department of Anthropology, University of Texas, Austin.

1984   Investigaciones en la cuenca del Lucre, Cusco. *Gaceta arqueológica andina* 9:12–15.

1987   *The Middle Horizon in the Valley of Cuzco, Peru: The impact of the Wari occupation of Pikillacta in the Lucre Basin.* BAR International Series 372, British Archaeological Reports, Oxford, England.

Matienzo, Juan de

1910   *Gobierno del Perú* [1567]. Buenos Aires: Compañía Sud-Americana de Billetes de Banco.

Menzel, Dorothy A.

1959   The Inca occupation of the south coast of Peru. *Southwestern Journal of Anthropology* 15 (2): 125–142.

Meyers, Albert
   1975   Algunos problemas en la clasificacíon del estilo incaico. *Pumapunku* 8:7–25.

Miller, Joseph C.
   1980   Introduction: Listening for the African past. In *The African past speaks*. London: W. and J. Machay.

Molina (de Cuzco), Cristóbal de
   1943   Relación de las fábulas y ritos de los Incas [1575]. In *Las cronicas de los Molinas*. Los Pequeños Grandes Libros de Historia Americana, series 1, vol. 4. Lima: Imprenta D. Miranda.

Morris, Craig
   1967   *Storage in Tawantinsuyu*. Ph. D. diss., Department of Anthropology, University of Chicago.
   1971   The identification of function in provincial Inca architecture and ceramics. In *Actas y memorias del XXXIX congreso internacional de americanistas* 3:135–144. Lima: Instituto de Estudios Peruanos. Also published in *Revista del Museo Nacional* 37.
   1972   State settlements in Tawantinsuyu: A strategy of compulsory urbanism. In *Contemporary archaeology: A guide to theory and contributions*. Edited by M. P. Leone, pp. 393–401. Carbondale: Southern Illinois University Press.
   1974   Reconstructing patterns of non-agricultural production in the Inca economy: Archaeology and ethnohistory in institutional analysis. In *The reconstruction of complex societies*. Edited by C. B. Moore, pp. 49–68. Philadelphia: American Schools of Oriental Research.
   1978   The archaeological study of Andean exchange systems. In *Social archaeology: Beyond subsistence and dating*. Edited by C. L. Redman, M. J. Berman, E. V. Curtin, W. T. Langhorne, Jr., N. M. Versaggi, and J. C. Wanser, pp. 315–337. New York: Academic Press.
   1982   The infrastructure of Inka control in the Peruvian central highlands. In *The Inca and Aztec states, 1400–1800: Anthropology and history*. Edited by G. A. Collier et al., pp. 153–171. New York: Academic Press.
   1988   Progress and prospect in the archaeology of the Inca. In *Peruvian prehistory*. Edited by R. Keatinge, pp. 233–256. Cambridge: Cambridge University Press.

Morris, Craig, and Donald E. Thompson
   1985   *Huánuco Pampa: An Inca city and its hinterland*. London: Thames and Hudson.

Muelle, Jorge C.
   1945   Pacarectambo: Apuntes de viaje. *Revista del Museo Nacional* 14:153–160.

Murra, John V.
   1962   An archaeological "restudy" of an Andean ethnohistorical account. *American Antiquity* 28:1–4.
   1968   An Aymara kingdom in 1567. *Ethnohistory* 15 (2): 115–151.
   1970   Current research and prospects in Andean ethnohistory. *Latin American Research Review* 5 (1): 3–36.

1972   El "control vertical" de un máximo de pisos ecológicos en la economía de las sociedades andinas. In *Visita de la provincia de León de Huánuco*, pp. 429–476. Huánuco, Peru: Universidad Nacional Hermilio Valdizán.

1980   *The economic organization of the Inca state* [1955]. Greenwich, Conn.: JAI Press.

1984   Andean societies before 1532. In *Cambridge history of Latin America*, vol. 1, pp. 59–90. Cambridge: Cambridge University Press.

Murra, John V., and Craig Morris

1976   Dynastic oral tradition, administrative records and archaeology in the Andes. *World Archaeology* 7 (3): 267–279.

Murúa, Martín de

1962   *Historia general del Perú, origen y descendencia de los Incas* . . . [1615]. Edited by M. Ballesteros-Garbrois, 2 vols. Biblioteca Americana Vetus. Madrid: Instituto Gonzalo Fernández de Oviedo.

Netherly, Patricia J.

1984   The management of late Andean irrigation systems on the north coast of Peru. *American Antiquity* 49 (2): 227–254.

Netherly, Patricia J., and Tom Dillehay

1986   Duality in public architecture in the Upper Zaña Valley, northern Peru. In *Perspectives on Andean prehistory and protohistory*. Edited by D. H. Sandweiss and D. P. Kvietok, pp. 85–97. Ithaca, N.Y.: Cornell Latin American Studies Program.

Niles, Susan A.

1980   *Civil and social engineers: Inca planning in the Cuzco region*. Ann Arbor, Mich.: University Microfilms.

1987   *Callachaca: Style and status in an Inca community*. Iowa City: University of Iowa Press.

O'Neale, Lila M.

1977   Notes on pottery making in highland Peru. *Ñawpa Pacha* 14:41–59.

Orton, Colin G.

1980   *Mathematics in archaeology*. Cambridge: Cambridge University Press.

Pachacuti Yamqui Salcamayhua, Juan de Santa Cruz

1950   Relación de antigüedades deste Reyno del Perú [1613]. In *Tres relaciones de antigüedades peruanas*. Edited by M. Jiménez de la Espada, pp. 207–281. Asunción del Paraguay: Editora Guaranía.

Pardo, Luis A.

1938   Hacia una nueva clasificación de la cerámica cuzqueña del antiguo imperio de los Incas, Perú. *Revista del Instituto Arqueológico del Cusco* 3 (4–5): 1–22.

1939   Arte peruano: Clasificación de la cerámica cuzqueña (época incaica). *Revista de la Sección Arqueológica de la Universidad Nacional del Cuzco* 4 (6–7): 3–27.

1946   La metrópoli de Paccarictambu: El adoratorio de tamputtocco y el itinerario del camino seguido por los hermanos ayar. *Revista del Instituto Arqueológico del Cuzco* 2:2–46.

1957   *Historia y arqueología del Cuzco.* 2 vols. Callao, Peru: Imprenta del Colegio Militar Leonico Prado.

Parsons, Jeffrey R.

1972   Archaeological settlement patterns. *Annual Review of Anthropology* 1:127–150.

Parsons, Jeffrey R., and Charles M. Hastings

1977   Prehispanic settlement patterns in the Upper Mantaro, Peru. A progress report for the 1976 field season. Unpublished report submitted to the Instituto Nacional de Cultura, Lima, and the National Science Foundation, Washington, D.C.

1988   The Late Intermediate Period. In *Peruvian prehistory.* Edited by R. W. Keatinge, pp. 190–229. Cambridge: Cambridge University Press.

Patterson, Thomas C.

1985   Exploitation and class formation in the Inca state. *Culture* 5 (1): 35–42.

Pease, Franklin Y.

1982   The formation of Tawantinsuyu: Mechanisms of colonization and relationship with ethnic groups. In *The Inca and Aztec states, 1400–1800: Anthropology and history.* Edited by G. Collier et al., pp. 173–198. New York: Academic Press.

Pizzaro, Pedro

1921   *Relation of the discovery and conquest of the kingdoms of Peru.* Translated and edited by C. R. Means. New York: Cortes Society.

Polo de Ondegardo, Juan

1916   *Relación de los fundamentos acerca del notable daño que resulta de no guardar a los Indios sus fueros* [1571]. Edited by H. Urteaga. Colección de Libros y Documentos Referentes a la Historia del Peru, series 1, vol. 3. Lima: Sanmartí.

Poole, Deborah

1984   *Ritual economic calendars in Paruro: The structure of representation in Andean ethnography.* Ann Arbor, Mich.: University Microfilms.

Pulgar Vidal, Javier

1967   *Geografía del Perú: Las ochos regiones naturales del Perú.* Lima: Editorial Universo.

Raimondi, Antonio

1874   *El Perú: Historia de la geografía del Perú* (Tomo I). Lima: Imprenta del Estado.

Ramos Gavilan, Alonso

1967   *Historia del Santuario de Nuestra Señora de Copacabana* [1621]. La Paz: Cámara Nacional de Comercio, Cámara Nacional de Industrias.

Renfew, Colin

1975   Trade as action at a distance. In *Ancient civilization and trade.* Edited by J. A. Sabloff and C. C. Lamberg-Karlovsky, pp. 3–59. Albuquerque: University of New Mexico Press.

Rice, Don, Charles Stanish, and Phillip R. Scarr, eds.
　1989　*Ecology, settlement and history in the Osmore Drainage, southern Peru.* BAR International Series 545, British Archaeological Reports, Oxford, England.

Rice, Prudence M.
　1987　*Pottery analysis: A source book.* Chicago: University of Chicago Press.

Ricoeur, Paul
　1980　*The contributions of French historiography to the theory of history.* Zaharoff Lectures. New York: Oxford University Press.

Rivera Dorado, Miguel
　1971a　La cerámica killke y la arqueología de Cuzco. *Revista española de antropología americana* 6:85–123.
　1971b　Diseños decorativos en la cerámica killke. *Revista del Museo Nacional* 37:106–115.
　1972　La cerámica de Cancha-Cancha, Cuzco, Perú. *Revista dominicana de arqueología y antropología* 2 (2–3): 36–49.
　1973　Aspectos tipológicos de la cerámica cuzqueña del Período Intermedio Tardío. In *Atti del 40 Congresso Internazionale degli Americanisti*, vol. 1, pp. 353–362. Rome-Genoa.

Rostworowski de Diez Canseco, María
　1970　Los Ayarmaca. *Revista del Museo Nacional* 36:58–101.
　1978　Una hipótesis sobre el surgimiento del estado inca. In *Actas y trabajos del III congreso peruano "El hombre y la cultura andina"* (Tomo 1). Edited by R. Matos M., pp. 89–100. Lima: Universidad Nacional Mayor de San Marcos.
　1988　*Historia del Tahuantinsuyu.* Lima: Instituto de Estudios Peruanos.

Rowe, John H.
　1944　An introduction to the archaeology of Cuzco. In *Papers of the Peabody Museum of American Archaeology and Ethnology*, vol. 27, no. 2. Cambridge, Mass.: Harvard University.
　1945　Absolute chronology in the Andean area. *American Antiquity* 10 (3): 265–284.
　1946　Inca culture at the time of the Spanish Conquest. In *Handbook of South American Indians*, vol. 2, *The Andean civilizations*. Edited by Julian Steward. *Bulletin of the Bureau of American Ethnology*, no. 143, pp. 183–330. Washington, D.C.: U.S. Government Printing Office.
　1956　Archaeological explorations in southern Peru, 1954–1955. *American Antiquity* 22 (2): 135–150.
　1957　La arqueología del Cuzco como historia cultural. *Revista del Museo e Instituto Histórico del Cuzco* 10 (16–17): 34–48.
　1962　Stages and periods in archaeological interpretation. *Southwestern Journal of Anthropology* 18 (1): 40–54.
　1967a　An interpretation of radiocarbon measurements on archaeological samples from Peru. In *Peruvian archaeology: Selected readings.*

Edited by J. H. Rowe and D. Menzel, pp. 16–30. Palo Alto, Calif.: Peek Publications.

1967b   What kind of settlement was Inca Cuzco? *Ñawpa Pacha* 5:59–75.

1970   La arqueología del Cuzco como historia cultural. In *100 anos de arqueología en el Perú*. Edited by Rogger Ravines, pp. 490–563. Lima: Instituto de Estudios Peruanos y Petróleos del Perú.

1985   La constitución inca del Cuzco. *Histórica* 9 (1): 35–73.

Sahlins, Marshall

1983   Other times, other customs: The anthropology of history. *American Anthropologist* 85:517–544.

1985   *Islands of history*. Chicago: University of Chicago Press.

Salas de Coloma, Miriam

1979   *De los obrajes de Canaria y Chincheros a las comunidades indígenas de Vilcashuaman, Siglo XVI*. Lima: Moncloa Editores.

Santa Cruz Pachacuti Yamqui Salcamayhua, Juan de. *See* Pachacuti Yamqui Salcamayhua, Juan de Santa Cruz.

Sarmiento de Gamboa, Pedro

1906   Segunda parte de la historia general llamada Indica ... [1572]. In *Geschichte des Inkareiches von Pedro Sarmiento de Gamboa*. Edited by Richard Pietschmann. Abhandlungen der Königlichen Gesellschaft der Wissenschaften zu Göttingen, Philologisch-Historische Klasse, vol. 6, no. 4. Berlin: Weidmannsche Buchhandlung.

Schaedel, Richard P.

1978   Early state of the Incas. In *The early state*. Edited by H. J. M. Claessen and P. Skalnik, pp. 289–320. The Hague: Mouton.

Schreiber, Katharina J.

1987   Conquest and consolidation: A comparison of the Wari and Inka occupation of a highland Peruvian valley. *American Antiquity* 52 (2): 266–284.

Seler, Eduard

1893   *Peruanische Alterthümer, insbesondere altperuanische Gefasse* ... Berlin: E. Mertens.

Seligmann, Linda

1987   *Land, labor and power: Local initiative and land reform in Huanoquite, Peru*. Ann Arbor, Mich.: University Microfilms.

Sherbondy, Jeanette

1982   *The canal systems of Hanan Cuzco*. Ann Arbor, Mich.: University Microfilms.

Squier, George E.

1877   *Peru: Incidents of travel and exploration in the land of Incas*. New York: Harper and Brothers.

Stanish, Charles n.d. Archaeological research at Juli, Peru. Manuscript on file in the Field Museum of National History, Chicago.

Stuiver M., and P. J. Reimer

1986   Programs Calib and Display. *Radiocarbon* 28:1022–1030.

Thompson, Donald E.
1968a Incaic installations at Huánuco and Pumpu. In *Actas y memorias del XXXVII congreso internacional de americanistas*, vol. 1, pp. 67–74. Mar del Plata, Argentina.
1968b An archaeological evaluation of ethnohistoric evidence on Inca culture. In *Anthropological archaeology in the Americas*. Edited by B. Meggers, pp. 108–120. Washington, D.C.: Anthropological Society of Washington, D.C.
1968c Huanuco Peru: A survey of a province of the Inca Empire. *Archaeology* 21 (3): 174–181.

Toledo, Francisco de
1920 *Informaciones sobre el antiguo Perú* [1572–1575]. Colección de Libros y Documentos Referentes a la Historia del Peru, series 2a, vol. 3. Lima: Sanmartí.
1975 *Tasa de la visita general de Francisco de Toledo*. Edited by Noble David Cook. Lima: Universidad Nacional Mayor de San Marcos, Seminario de Historia Rural Andina.

Topic, John R., and Theresa L. Topic
1983 Huamachuco archaeological project: preliminary report on the second season, June–August 1982. Manuscript in possession of the author.

Torres Poblete, Nilo
1989 Sondeo arqueológico de Araway. Licenciado en Arqueologia Tesis, Facultad de Ciencias Sociales, Universidad Nacional San Antonio Abad del Cusco.

Tosi, Joseph A.
1960 *Zonas de vida natural en el Perú: Memoria explicativa sobre el mapa ecológica del Perú*. Instituto Interamericano de Ciencias Agrícolas de la OEA Zona Andina, Boletin Técnico, no. 5. Lima: Organización de Estados Americanos.

Troll, Carl
1968 The cordilleras of the tropical Americas: Aspects of climate, phytogeographical and agrarian ecology. In *Geo-Ecology of the mountainous regions of the tropical Americas/Geo-ecología de las regiones montañosas*. Mexico Symposium (1966). Edited by C. Troll, vol. 9, pp. 15–56. Bonn: F. Dummlers Verlag.

Turner, Terence S.
1984 Dual opposition, hierarchy and value: Moiety structure and symbolic polarity in central Brazil and elsewhere. In *Différences, valeurs, hiérarchie: Textes offerts a Louis Dumont et réunis par Jean-Claude Galey*. Edited by Jean-Claude Galey, pp. 335–370. Paris: Éditions de l'École des Hautes Études en Sciences Sociales.
1988 Ethno-ethnohistory: Myth and history in native South American representations of contact with western society. In *Rethinking history and myth: Indigenous South American perspectives on the past*. Edited by Jonathan D. Hill, pp. 235–281. Urbana: University of Illinois Press.

Uhle, Max

1912   Los orígenes de los Incas. In *Actas del XVII congreso internacional de americanistas*, pp. 302–352. Buenos Aires.

Ulloa, Luis

1909   Documentos del Virrey Toledo: Visita general de los yndios del Cuzco, año de 1571, provincia Condesuyo. *Revista histórica* 2:332–347.

Urbano, Henrique

1981   *Wiracocha y Ayar: Héroes y funciones en las sociedades andinas.* Cuzco: Centro de Estudios Rurales Andinos, "Bartolomé de Las Casas."

Urton, Gary D.

1984   Chuta: El espacio de la práctica social en Pacariqtambo, Perú. *Revista andina* 2 (1): 7–56.

1985   Animal metaphors and the life cycle in an Andean community. In *Animal myths and metaphors in South America: An anthology.* Edited by. G. Urton, pp. 251–284. Salt Lake City: University of Utah Press.

1986   Calendrical cycles and their projections in Pacariqtambo, Peru. *Journal of Latin American Lore* 12 (1): 45–64.

1988   La arquitectura pública como texto social: La historia de un muro de adobe en Pacariqtambo, Perú (1915–1985). *Revista andina* 6 (1): 225–261.

1989   La historia de un mito: Pacariqtambo y el origen de los Incas. *Revista andina* 7 (1): 129–216.

1990   *The history of a myth: Pacariqtambo and the origin of the Inkas.* Austin: University of Texas Press.

Vaca de Castro, Cristóbal

1920   Discurso sobre la descendencia y gobierno de los Incas . . . [1542]. Colección de Libros y Documentos Referentes a la Historia del Perú, series 2a, vol. 3. Lima: Sanmartí.

Valcárcel Vizquerra, Luis E.

1934   Los trabajos arqueológicos del Cusco. Sajsawaman redescubierto II. *Revista del Museo Nacional* 3:3–36, 211–233.

1935   Los trabajos arqueológicos en el departamento del Cusco. Sajsawaman redescubierto III–IV. *Revista del Museo Nacional* 4:1–24, 161–203.

Valencia Zegarra, Alfredo I.

1970   Las tumbas de Saqsaywaman. *Saqsaywaman* 1:173–177.

Villanueva Urteaga, Horacio

1982   *Cuzco 1689: Economía y sociedad en el sur andino.* Cuzco: Centro de Estudios Rurales Andinos, "Bartolomé de Las Casas."

Weberbauer, August

1945   *El mundo vegetal de los Andes peruanos.* Lima: Estación Experimental Agrícola de la Molina, Ministerio de Agricultura.

Webster, Steven S.
  1971 An indigenous Quechua community in exploitation of multiple eco-
       logical zones. *Actas y memorias del XXXIX congreso internacional
       de americanistas* 3:174–183. Lima: Instituto de Estudios Peruanos.
  1973 Native pastoralism in the South Andes. *Ethnology* 12 (2): 115–133.
Wedin, Åke
  1963 *La cronología de la historia incaica.* Madrid: Instituto Ibero-Amer-
       icano Gotemburgo Suecia.
Wilson, David J.
  1988 *Prehispanic settlement patterns in the Lower Santa Valley, Peru.*
       Washington, D.C.: Smithsonian Institution Press.
Wright, Henry T., and Gregory A. Johnson
  1975 Population, exchange, and early state formation in southwestern
       Iran. *American Anthropologist* 77:267–289.
Yábar Moreno, Jorge
  1972 Época pre-Inca de Chanapata. *Revista Saqsaywaman* 2:211–233.
  1982 Figurillas de la cultura pre-Inka del Cuzco. In *Arqueología de
       Cuzco.* Compiled by Italo Oberti Rodríguez, pp. 9–12. Cuzco: In-
       stituto Nacional de Cultura.
Yamamoto, Norio
  1982 A food production system in the southern central Andes. *Senri
       Ethnological Studies* 10:39–57.
Zuidema, R. Tom
  1964 *The ceque system of Cuzco: The social organization of the capital
       of the Inca.* Leiden: E. J. Brill.
  1977 The Inca kinship: A new theoretical view. In *Andean kinship and
       marriage.* Edited by R. Bolton and E. Mayer. Special Publication
       no. 7, pp. 240–281. Washington, D.C.: American Anthropological
       Association.
  1980 El Ushnu. *Revista de la Universidad Complutense de Madrid* 28
       (117): 317–362.
  1982 Myth and history in ancient Peru. In *The logic of culture: Advances
       in structural theory and methods.* Edited by I. Rossi, pp. 150–175.
       South Hadley, Mass.: J. F. Bergin.
  1983 Hierarchy and space in Incaic social organization. *Ethnohistory* 30
       (2): 49–75.
  1986 *La civilisation Inca au Cuzco.* Collège de France, Essais et Confé-
       rences. Préface de F. Héritier-Augé. Paris: Presses Universitaires de
       France.
Zuidema, R. Tom, and Deborah Poole
  1982 Los límites de los cuatro suyus incaicos en el Cuzco. *Bulletin de
       l'Institut Français des Études Andines* 11 (1–2): 83–89.

Index